CW00553077

# The Coorie Home

## Beautiful Scottish Living

**BETH PEARSON**

**CIARA MENZIES**

BLACK & WHITE PUBLISHING

First published 2019
by Black & White Publishing Ltd
Nautical House, 104 Commercial Street,
Edinburgh, EH6 6NF

1 3 5 7 9 10 8 6 4 2   19 20 21 22

ISBN: 978 1 78530 267 1

Layout by creativelink.tv
Printed and bound in Spain by Estella Print

For my grandparents,
who welcomed all into their home.
**George and Eva Irvine**
1937–2018

# Contents

# Where d'You Stay?

Location, structure, culture

**1**

Everyone loves an icebreaker, especially in Scotland. Whether you are at the bus stop, on a night out in the pub, stopping off at a local café or making small talk at the swing park – we can all expect to be asked this simple and very Scottish question: 'Where d'you stay?'

But you can't always give a simple answer. You might be renting while renovating, a growing trend. You might be studying, caring or working in a location different to the address on your driving licence. Nevertheless, whether Scots by birth or association, we all seem to share the need to personalise the space in which we sleep, eat and repeat. To introduce *The Coorie Home* I'd like to create a panoramic view of Scottish home life – ranging from an array of living spaces today, to the earliest homes in Scotland. I trust that in doing so we will come to appreciate the deep-rootedness of the essence of coorie living.

# WHAT IS COORIE?

For me, coorie encompasses the Scottish inclination to welcome all. This welcoming approach is evident in how many trademarks of Scotland are fusions of cultures and origins, such as the Glaswegian accent, bagpipes and woollen clothing. Coorie is not a concept dependent on class or wealth; it is a lived experience available to everyone who would like to adopt it as their own. I love how the very word 'coorie' feels easy for natives and non-natives to pronounce, both sounding pleasingly Scottish when doing so.

Coorie also reflects the Scottish tendency to keep busy while at the same time finding a quiet moment to sit with a cup of tea; it can be a way to be cosy and ambitious within the same space. And, for me, the idea of coorie living favours the indoors and the outdoors equally, ultimately seeking to make the most of what comes from Scotland and aiming to be satisfied, too, with what already exists around you.

## WHAT DOES LIVING IN SCOTLAND LOOK LIKE?

Arguably, some people are now turning away from the big city to find somewhere less urban to put down roots. I've heard it said that Generation Z-ers are not so bothered with ready access to a thriving club scene and are more attracted to the low costs and gentler lifestyles of smaller towns and cities across Scotland. For example, BBC's 'The Social', an award-winning digital platform based in Glasgow, commissions content from all corners of Scotland. It has specifically highlighted local life in places such as Shetland, where comedian, improviser and storyteller Marjolein Robertson has shared the ins and outs, highs and lows of island life since 2017. I like to think it's no coincidence that the number of annual visitors to Shetland has increased by 8,500 in the last four years!

Conversely, urban living still prospers in Scotland. Areas of Dundee, Edinburgh and Glasgow, for example, are donning fresh, innovative personalities – changing up their tried-and-tested characteristics – partly driven by the welcome influx of 21st-century newcomers. It seems these shifts in a city's character can sit happily alongside their original traits too. One thing unites all of Scotland from top to tail: people have been surviving and thriving in unique, interconnected ways for thousands of years.

**Given our country's temperament**, I'd argue the most coorie element of inhabiting Scotland is finding shelter from the elements. Home as respite from the bitter cold, or roaring wind on the coast or mountaintops, as well as the infamous relentless rain. Scotland is stereotypically seen as a place replete with historical estates and wild refuges such as bothies. This external view of Scotland is perhaps perpetuated by its portrayal in dramas such as the TV show *Outlander*. And it's true there are majestic homes all over the country, atmospheric with history, where you can spend time for the right price, or with the right connections. Indeed, it is a unique experience, walking the halls of

Coorie Bookshelf

*Findings*
Kathleen Jamie

a grand Scottish home, connecting with the history that has gone before you.

The great thing about coorie living is that many of the delights of a luxurious time spent in such a place – a roaring fire, a cashmere blanket and a glass of something invigorating – can be replicated in much more everyday homes. And it's always good to enjoy these coorie pleasures without suffering the consequent humongous heating and maintenance bills of a castle of your own!

## THE ADAPTIVE COORIE HOME

It's worth noting that, with the evolving economic climate, living situations, patterns and plans are ever-changing. It is often now more common to live at your family home for longer. Sharing not only a roof but also sometimes a room is a reality – particularly in densely packed urban environments where space is at a premium – for many students and young professionals.

Alternative living situations such as shipping containers, renovated industrial spaces or vehicles and boats are becoming increasingly popular as housing and rent prices soar. These factors encourage people to get creative with a lack of space. Coorie living in such alternative living spaces brings a whole new meaning to cosiness.

**Alternative living spaces** are often glamorised, but people frequently seek them out of necessity. Jay, a houseboat owner based in Ratho, ten miles along the canal from Edinburgh, told me how he didn't want to rent so instead he bought a cheap canal boat, did it up for less than the price of a year's rent and now lives on it. He initially pretended it was for environmental reasons (and to an extent it was), but mainly it was a financial decision. What appeals to him now is that this way of life is efficient and simple. After moving from one temporary dwelling to another, the boat seems enormous and luxurious. Not to mention permanent and his own to inhabit as he chooses.

The small space means there's less to heat, clean, buy, manage, maintain, and it forces a certain level of practicality and organisation. When you arrive home with the shopping, you have to put it straight away. No point stopping for a cuppa, as you just put the shopping down where you normally sit. Jay finds it hard to pinpoint what makes his canal-based home feel specifically Scottish but he says there is something magical about being close to the weather, but warm and cosy beside a fire. This feeling of being snug while moored close to the surface of the canal, with trees densely green along the towpath, encapsulates that coorie notion of favouring both the outside and inside within your home.

# SHARING'S CARING

In a modern society that seems more in thrall to the impersonality of capitalism than a neighbour's simple need for help, a reliance on others sometimes feels quieter than the drive to be independent. In a lot of new developments in Scotland, roads are wider, as are spaces between properties. Many new housing estates are created without centres for communities, play areas, schools or even a local shop to buy your groceries. You can see how these residential landscapes might make it difficult to connect with neighbours and the wider community. However, alternative living situations such as repurposed developments, shared living spaces or mobile homes tend to make individual inhabitants more reliant on and engaged with their neighbours; in short, more connected to them.

**Evolving living situations** such as young adults staying at home for longer also result in different levels of effective and practical living. I remember one of my friends, who shared a room until she was 25, saying that the lack of space drove her to be more minimal and focused with her wardrobe. It also encouraged her and her roommate to share furniture such as

desks and drawers in order to conserve space. 'Clever' furniture was key, too. For example, a footstool/coffee table that opens up to reveal storage space and a drop-leaf dining-room table brought out for special occasions. The aim of this act of sharing was to save money for the household in terms of rent and utilities, but there are ways in which it also speaks to the history of Scottish living.

The realities of Scottish urban housing – from the crises of the early 1900s to the right-to-buy schemes of the 1980s – mean many families today live in quite straightforward, minimal conditions. From a coorie perspective, spaces are very lived-in. What you see is what you get. Like my friend's situation, her wee ex-council house isn't pretending to be anything it isn't. For me, something about the vulnerability of this makes it feel distinctly Scottish.

The intimacy of the shared home makes it very cosy, especially when there are fewer rooms and a more snug environment. When someone else is in, you are automatically sharing time and space with them, which in a larger home you could easily choose not to do. Again, I believe this concept of living close to, and comfortably alongside others is one that's prevalent in Scottish history.

## OLD-SCHOOL SCOTLAND

From the Mesolithic period we know that Scottish folk have always lived snugly side by side. The oldest shelter known in Scotland was a small oval structure of wooden posts, dating from around 8240 BCE, uncovered in north Edinburgh, during building works for the Queensferry Crossing in 2011. Stone structures have been found from as long ago as 6000 BCE, mostly in the Northern and Western Isles, where a lack of trees meant most edifices were built of local stone. We can visualise a clear picture of these ancient communities, adapting to brave the elements by living in squat structures.

**The Knap of Howar** on the island of Papa Westray in Orkney, is a Neolithic farmstead that is still remarkably intact. The fertile soil of the island has attracted people for thousands of years – radiocarbon dating proves the farmstead was occupied from 3700 to 2800 BCE. Today you can visit the site and experience the vivid impression the stone furniture gives of life in the ancient home. Fireplaces, partition screens, beds and storage shelves feel close to pristine. The roof structure is indicated by post-holes found at the site. I guess all these elements that have endured the centuries could have been the Stone Age interpretation of 'clever furniture'.

**From the Stone Age** we can find the concept of coorie illustrated in homes above – and perhaps below – ground. And, moving through the centuries, we can read Robert Burns' variations of the word 'coorie' to describe the action of folding or bending in the witches' dance in his poem 'Tam o' Shanter'. On a practical level, in certain climates, keeping things low to the ground can help conserve heat. This aspect of Scottish coorie is reflected globally in the ancient traditions of living in igloos, tents and tepees (which were much lower to the ground than the models we see today

might indicate). This Scottish way of connecting with, and indeed sometimes living in, the earth forged a bond with the natural landscapes of Scotland that we still value today.

**In the Scottish Iron Age**, multi-storey homes emerged from the creation of brochs (which are classified as 'complex Atlantic roundhouses'). Brochs typically had inner and outer walls that functioned as insulation but also, by connecting slabs, formed stairways to different floors of the building. Over time, these structures were repurposed for many

domestic, military and industrial uses. They are impressive, intriguing structures – well worth a visit if you happen to be near one of the many scattered throughout Scotland. Their origin is still debated, but it could be argued that they instigated a pattern in Scottish – and international – living of regeneration that is very much around today.

## INDUSTRIAL REALITIES

If we jump forward to the 19th century and then into the mid-20th century, we see a huge growth in Scotland's towns and cities thanks to the Industrial Revolution. Glasgow, for instance, expanded in all directions to attempt to house the factories and workers it was attracting. The attributes of the city's geology were capitalised upon, producing the instantly recognisable tenements in yellow and red sandstone that are present today. The majesty of the buildings from this period still acts as a mask for its many dark realities; one such being that the majority of the money fuelling Scottish success was made at the terrible expense of enslaved people who worked those tobacco, sugar and cotton plantations owned and run by Scots.

Another consequence of the city as a source of wealth for some was that the demand for workers fast overtook the housing capacity in Glasgow especially, creating dire living conditions for the majority of the working-class population.

Nevertheless, this period shaped Scotland into the country we know today. For example, Irish immigrants formed the majority of the workforce and populated large areas of Glasgow's city centre. Thus, they contributed to the Glaswegian accent, as their dialect fused with the locals and people who had moved down from the Highlands to make a living.

In addition, this huge shift in industry radically changed the landscapes of Scotland's largest cities. After the heavy industries were shut down or exported out of Scotland, we were left with vast swathes of abandoned, de-industrialised areas lacking their original purpose. And here, I believe, the Scottish mindset has set itself the task of what it often does best: making the most of what is already present.

Some might see old factories and warehouses as reminders of a redundant past that need to be removed. However, the regeneration of many industrial areas of Scottish cities such as Leith, Finnieston and Glasgow's East End has given incredible new life to dilapidated structures in many different ways. In both Glasgow and Edinburgh, factories such as that of the Scottish Adhesives Company, now the Glue Factory, have been rebirthed into thriving arts spaces that enable each city's current significant export of culture.

Coorie Bookshelf

*Red Dust Road*
Jackie Kay

# Leith
## a case study

In Leith, we see old shipping premises and warehouses blossoming into urban housing and opportunities for new businesses to thrive. With rent prices in Leith originally being a fraction of those in Edinburgh's city centre for commercial and domestic spaces, people have flocked to the former port since the early 2000s, bolstering and reinvigorating the community there. The diversity and eclectic atmosphere of the area is testament to a coorie mindset.

Since 2001 there has been a significant growth of population in the areas surrounding Leith Walk (an increase of up to 30%), as a result of new house building on brownfield land, together with refurbishment of existing properties. It could be said that the area showcases a clever use of space as, with a peak of nearly 26,000 people residing within an 800-metre radius, Leith has a higher local population density than anywhere else in Scotland, including Glasgow. At its best, this is a situation that leads to all sorts of coorie opportunities.

Historically, Leith was a separate burgh – with a distinct boundary – until it merged with the rest of Edinburgh in 1920. Yes, it is heralded as the place that Mary, Queen of Scots landed on arrival in Scotland, but Leith has always been known for the energy of its ordinary folk who worked what was once Scotland's premier port. Their skills and trades are recognised in place names such as Fishmarket Square, Whale Brae and Baltic Street. However, like Glasgow's East End, Leith was characterised by the unhealthy living conditions caused by overpopulation – and poverty – until the late 1980s, the reality of which is still present for some. The area retains its particular atmosphere and topography, along with a fierce sense of local pride; unlike the rest of Edinburgh, Leith lived and breathed industry. It is worth exploring the work of Edinburgh artists – for example, David McClure – who strove to capture this.

In common with post-industrial parts of Glasgow and Dundee, Leith has a diverse and ever-changing community. Early evidence of this can be seen in the Dutch and Germanic-inspired architecture that is so characteristic of The Shore. The 19th century saw Irish and Italian communities develop in Leith, and in the 20th century the area welcomed those seeking refuge from war, economic instability and political upheavals – or simply seeking a new life.

**Sir Eduardo Paolozzi**, a pioneer of pop art, was born in Leith. A symbol of the Italian migratory influence on the city, with pubs and beers named after him, I see the heft of Paolozzi's bold artistry most in the fusion of pop culture and industrial machinery in Leith. For me, these influences have helped the area hold on to its roots while it evolves with the constantly changing economic and cultural climates.

**As with alternative living, loft-style apartments and offices** are now coveted as high-end and desirable, despite their more lowly origins. The property and building professionals Whiteburn, worked with architect Gordon Duffy to create Scotland's first loft development in 1997, called 'The Shore', out of two dilapidated whisky bonds. 'From a home for pigeons, to a Golden Goose' was their fabulous tagline. More recently I discovered an Airbnb, also located in Leith, which markets itself as 'A New York Style Warehouse'. This – perhaps slightly ironic – reference nods to the origins of 'loft living', none of which were especially glamorous or chic, as well as the type of building found in Leith.

As with urban areas of Scotland, New York had to cope with a radical downsizing of industry, not to mention how the city has always had to contend with a pressing lack of space. While the wealthy commandeered large spaces in Manhattan for extortionate prices, broke artists such as the young Andy Warhol looked to the abandoned plots of Soho and Tribeca for cheap buildings to work and live in.

Just as in Scotland, more avant-garde culture and the arts were at the forefront of architectural trends. A link might be made, too, between the practice of grassroots regeneration – however edgy – born of necessity and some of the qualities of coorie living.

## A CONTRAST

Two polar-opposite residential concepts have recently been developed in and around Leith. Both illustrate coorie ideals, but in very different ways.

**The Social Bite Village**, based not far away in Granton, encapsulates how elements of the coorie home can be accessible for everybody. Approaching the small cluster of homes, you could mistake the village for a weekend haven, the sort of Highland retreat folk seek

out to recharge from the stresses of city living. There are posh soaps in the bathrooms, handcrafted blankets on the beds and rows of decorative plants splashing colour around neat, manicured gardens. In the distance, the sun dapples the Firth of Forth and wood pigeons gently bill and coo in the thicket of trees.

But these are not exclusive holiday homes. The people who live here are some of the most vulnerable members of society. The village facilitates a safe living environment for up to 20 people for around 12 to 18 months. It is the brainchild of the social enterprise, Social Bite, which runs cafés throughout Scotland. One in every four members of staff at these innovative, popular cafés have experienced homelessness.

Social Bite founder, Josh Littlejohn, says:

'We're not pretending this is a one-stop solution. But in Edinburgh alone there are 600 homeless people in B&Bs costing £6m a year, and yet there are pockets of vacant council-owned land.'

In addition, of course, to its essential purpose, the Social Bite Village embodies the ideals of the coorie home by being accessible in a practical and symbolic sense. Physically, each unit, built by donations from local businesses, makes effective use of space but creates, too, a real sense of personality. Social Bite has made use of the resources around them to create cosy, inhabitable spaces for those who need them most.

**The *Fingal*, docked in the historic port of Leith, sits at a very different place on the scale.** This ship was originally a lighthouse tender, whose task it was to transport crew and equipment to some of the most treacherous, inaccessible parts of Scotland. But recently the *Fingal* has been remodelled into a luxury boutique hotel by the award-winning team at the Royal Yacht Britannia. The ship's interior is imbued with her Scottish maritime heritage, with polished woods, nautical touches, Scottish leathers and a sea-inspired palette.

Each of the 23 suites is named after the famous Stevenson lighthouses, more than one hundred of which were designed by engineer Robert Stevenson and his descendants (including his grandson Robert Louis Stevenson). This contrasting style of temporary living is undeniably Scottish. It speaks of the booming Scottish food and drink industry,

with on-board bar and dining facilities that enhance the already vibrant selection available in Leith. This new venture also creates a coorie-style environment to stay in – reminiscent of grand Scottish estates, like Gleneagles, but fused with the industrial history of Leith.

The more controversial side of such expensive loveliness is that many fear that if Leith continues to head in this direction, then it will lose its own particular character. However, my hope is that the area continues to uphold this new balance of luxury and practicality. I trust it's the case that the coorie home is one that offers the same pleasures for all: a sanctuary from the harsh Scottish elements and the satisfaction that comes from continuing, adapting and re-imagining Scottish traditions in experimental times.

# Which Buzzer?

Entranceways and more

**2**

Scotland is small in size but large in variety. Some journeys are blessed with space – sprawling estates that entail a ten-minute drive to get to the inevitable grandeur of a front door. Whereas others are through narrow wynds, up ancient stairs and across landings, searching for the seemingly invisible Flat 2/4. The ways Scots have situated their homes speaks volumes and, over the centuries, the need for protection from enemy lines has merged into the need to not hear every word of a conversation outside – or upstairs – at two in the morning. This chapter focuses on key traits of the coorie home: driveways, façades, entrances, closes and front gardens – in short, what you see on approaching a Scottish home.

# FAÇADES

Scotland is a smorgasbord of architectural styles offering a range of key trends. A trend that is instantly recognisable – once you know to look for it – is the use of rough stone or rubble in constructing homes around Scotland.

And so it is that 'Rubblemania' has come to represent Scottish architecture internationally. This material has been used since the Mesolithic era – that is, over 10,000 years ago – and it is still used in Scottish buildings today. The use of rubble links a wide range of buildings throughout the centuries – from grand castles and estates such as Dunstaffnage Castle to Charles Rennie Mackintosh's unforgettable designs of the early 20th century to the architecture that developed across Scotland in the post-war era.

Stone is ideal for homes built to brave the weather. More waterproof than treated wood – a material seen often in other Northern European houses – rough stone walls can be finished with a lime render, or harled for complete weatherproofing and a uniform appearance. This creates a clear visual and aesthetic difference between homes that might be called coorie as opposed to hygge.

Originally a cheap and accessible construction form, rubble soon became a staple element in Scottish design, 'a manifesto of Scottishness'.[i] This material captures the essence of Scottish historic architecture and has since been used in every kind of housing. In this sense, although part of a broader European aesthetic, rough stone can be seen to represent a uniquely Scottish *ethic*.

Coorie Bookshelf

*A Sense of Place*
Joan Eardley

## ENTRANCEWAYS

Where some entranceways to our homes
are created along purely aesthetic lines,
most have at least an element of function-
ality. In the case of front-garden allotments
and, for the more adventurous, beekeeping, they can be used for production. Or, as
is the case for many of us, for storage.

'Drives' or driveways to our front doors
evolved from the paths people used to
reach their homes on foot. In an urban
context, they are something of a status
symbol, particularly in cities such as
Edinburgh where your own outdoor space
is at a premium. But typically, the more rural
your home, the more likely you are to have
a driveway that belongs to you alone. In a
countryside setting, access to your home
might involve fords, cattle grids, gates and
other features related to working on the
land or living alongside those who do.

In city environments, or for homes
facing on to busy roads, Scottish councils
often enforce features such as 'car turn-
tables' in a bid to reduce traffic accidents.
These extraordinary devices are genius
when it comes to maximising spaces
almost too small to house a car. They
also make excellent spectator sport. My
morning coffee when I lived in Glasgow's
West End was enlivened by watching a
neighbour, who'd renovated his tenement
backhouse, rotate his car before he set off
for work.

# FRONT GARDENS

Before the Industrial Revolution, most ordinary people used any outdoor space they had to grow their own produce. Then, for generations, the short-back-and-sides front garden – where there was one – became more of the norm. However, with increasing work hours and more pressing commitments, people might opt for the low-maintenance approach and pave or gravel their front gardens in the shape of extended driveways. Plant pots and ornaments such as gnomes and windmills have become popular as ways to create witty, colourful focal points in your garden and drive without breaking the bank or doing serious landscaping!

But perhaps there is a happy medium between form and function. I like to think that the notion of 'respectable' evolves with every generation.

> "Perhaps your grandparents would walk by a front garden of millimetre-trimmed, bright green lawn, surrounded by precisely equidistant bedding plants, and nod with approval. You on the other hand might walk by a front garden clearly arranged to attract bees and birds, and similarly feel: this householder adheres to the current consensus view of good values.[ii]"

MAT COWARD, GARDENING COLUMNIST

And so it is that gardens are developing from the 'prim and proper' to a more free-flowing, ethical and practical usage – signalling something of a return to the pre-Industrial Revolution approach. As society becomes more aware of climate change, any small change or step towards sustainability that one can make in or around the home can feel like progress.

Mat Coward talks about a growing impetus to cultivate your own fruit and veg in your front garden as a 'small way of repairing the environment'.[iii]

**Restrictive covenants** are when property builders place restrictions on what buyers can do with or to their homes. These are nothing new and are similar to conservation restrictions on older properties. Recently some covenants have made the headlines thanks to the absurdity of banning washing lines, cats and sheds! With these restrictions in place in housing developments and conservation areas – there to maintain a uniformity of appearance from one home to the next – often the addition of allotments needs to be so super discreet as to be 'invisible'. But creative ways round bureaucracy can always be found – in this case by planting and nurturing 'ornamentals' that you can also eat.

Propagate, a Glasgow collective, are geniuses at growing produce in small spaces. By reflecting the city itself and building upwards when there is a lack of space, with 'micro forests', which look like green tower blocks, they show how we can overcome restrictions whether environmental or legislative.

## HI HONEY, I'M HOME

Beekeeping is another clever, resource-ful way of making the most out of small amounts of land. Bees are essential to the growth of plants, and so the keeping of bees supports the Scottish ecosystem. Scottish urban beekeeping has enjoyed something of a recent resurgence, but it's a practice that has deep historical roots in Scotland. The box hive, which is widely used today, was first patented in Scotland in 1651.

In Glasgow, members of the Glasgow and District Beekeepers' Association often keep bees hidden in plain sight at the front of tenements. Apparently, neighbours don't even notice until you hand them a jar of 100% local honey! I'm told that rooftops and car parks are also ideal locations for urban beekeeping.

Most bees are related to the Scottish Honeybee. Urban beekeeper Ed O'Brien and executive chef Zoltan Szabo of Blythswood Square Hotel, Glasgow favour a specific strain called the Bucky Bee, bred at Buckfast Abbey in the 1920s. The Bucky Bee is surprisingly mellow, despite the high caffeine content of its namesake.

## DOORS

Research has established a clear link between the quality of your environment, your interactions with it and your mental health. Refining housing features such as front doors is recognised to benefit physical and mental health.[iv]

A study led by academics from the University of Glasgow revealed how the front door can represent both the security and the personality of your home. For example, painting your front door translates your approach to interior style to the outside of your home. And when that front door is visible to passers-by it can communicate many things to those who choose to look.

The hanging of a wreath can symbolise a celebration of Christmas; a bower of orange flowers a Sikh wedding. It's a delight to see a neighbourly symbiosis when a cluster of houses coordinates the colour schemes of their front doors.

As well as the more traditional doormat, many homes in Scotland have facilities similar to those found at golf clubs, to scrape mud off your footwear before entering the home. This almost ritualistic removal of the earth speaks of the deep connection Scottish homes have always had to the land.

# ALL ABOUT DOORS
## A ROUND-UP

Northern Irish illustrator Alison Soye, who stays in Edinburgh, is known for her fascination with beautiful front doors. As we wandered through a wee back street between Bonnington and Broughton, she explained what intrigues her about them and what she has become aware of through her art and her photography.

**What intrigues you about front doors, specifically in Scotland?**
How people 'dress them' in different ways – painting their doors, adding beautiful door numbers, creating leading lanes and quirky gates. I also love how the doors are often adapted to seasons and events – for example, Christmas and autumn wreaths, Halloween decorations and even balloons for birthdays. I feel that in a lot of areas in Scotland people take pride in their front doors, as it's their one way to make a leading impression on their home.

**What do you think you can learn about a person from to their front door?**
I think you can learn a lot about a person's creative mind by how their front door looks! For instance, they might have a really bright,

colourful paint colour on their door if they have a loud personality. A traditional doorway might show a person appreciates the history and heritage of their country. An uncared-for doorway, and peeling paint, might show that a person perhaps cannot afford or doesn't have the time to maintain it. Or perhaps it is just not a priority! You can sometimes see the opposite of this in the pride lots of retired people take in maintaining immaculate doorways and front gardens.

**What have you learned about Edinburgh and Scotland from studying and photographing doors?**
I have learned how traditional and historical Edinburgh and Scotland might have looked as many of the doors have been so well preserved. I have also learned how buildings

and doorways are very important in establishing a sense of pride in homes, businesses and historical, national buildings.

**How do you think someone could at a low cost improve their front door?**
Paint. Natural seasonal wreaths – holly, ivy, pine cones for Christmas; red and orange leaves and acorns for autumn; fresh green leaves for spring or summer.

Simply keeping the front door clean and clear of bins or debris can also make a big difference!

Coorie Bookshelf

*Katie Morag's Island Stories*
Mairi Hedderwick

## CATCH THE SUN

If you are planning on building your own home – or simply renting or buying a property – take a compass with you. The following rule of thumb was taken from the indigenous blackhouses that were still being built into the 19th century.

The positioning of the blackhouse was vital; it made a significant contribution to the warmth of the interior. Its rounded, narrow gable end faced the prevailing wind, and any openings, such as the door, were placed on the south-facing side towards the sun. You might prefer to swap things round, though, so your outside space, whether front garden, back yard or balcony, is the area that catches the sun's rare rays.

These blackhouse stipulations are echoed in the Gaelic proverb.[v]

*'An iar's an ear, an dachaigh as 'fhearr –*
*cul ri gaoith, 's aghaidh ri grein.'*

'East to west, the house that's best –
back to the wind and face to the sun.'

## FIRST FOOTING

A symbolic tradition of Scottish heritage is 'first footing'. This is when – so as to bless the household with good luck on New Year's Eve – people celebrating Hogmanay carry out a ritual involving a friend or guest. The person of choice retreats from the house, only then to knock and re-enter with symbolic gifts of coal, shortbread, salt, and a wee dram of whisky to bless the home and the new year. The coal in particular is often followed by the greeting 'Lang may yer lum reek!' which implies 'May you never be without fuel for your fire!', but more literally translates to 'Long may your chimney smoke!'

## CLOSE ENCOUNTERS

Up until 1700, in the older Scottish tongue, *coorie* or *ecurie* referred to the Royal Stables. This evolved into the concept we might recognise today: to stoop or crouch for protection, to nestle, to embrace. Similarly, another prominent Scottish term evolved to become central to many living situations: close. A 'close' was originally an enclosed space adjoining a house. Off the Royal Mile in Edinburgh are many fascinating closes that give a glimpse of what it would have been like in the medieval city. Situated

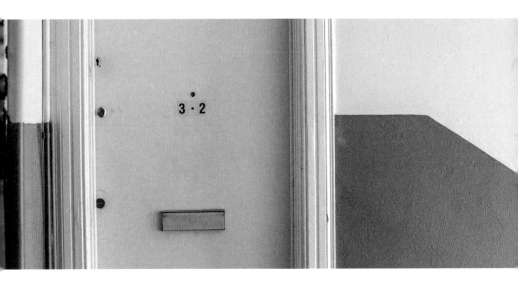

within the former town walls, they intentionally gave inhabitants protection and peace of mind, as they are framed with tall buildings and not well known to those who don't live there. Many of these closes have evocative names that speak of their former uses such as Fleshmarket Close and World's End Close. The meaning of the word 'close' later shifted to signify a central area which farm houses and buildings communed around. Nowadays, we think of it as a narrow alley or the communal stairwell of a block of tenement flats.

In industrialised cities in Scotland, there are a huge range of closes. A 'wally close', for example, was a sign of social superiority, as this meant the communal inside space was tiled with beautiful pale ceramics. The argument for tiling the stair was that it made upkeep and cleaning easier. While poorer tenement blocks had simple gloss paint adorning the walls – with darker paint below and paler above; again, the darker paint was there to disguise the scuff of boot- and hand-prints.

This is how a 'close' is defined in the Tenements (Scotland) Act 2004:

i. Be within a tenement building
ii. Include a stair or landing, and
iii. Constitute common access to two or more flats.

# CONTEMPORARY CLOSES

A tenement close is such a unique space. In every one I walk into – whether it's in Glasgow or Aberdeen – I am captivated by the unique tiling or paintwork. The other fascinating element of a close is how each resident chooses to utilise the space surrounding their front door. Whether it be a doormat with a welcoming slogan or a little note for the delivery man, a row of flowerpots on the banister or a hand-painted tile with a flat number, I find this personalisation speaks to the very human need to claim and personalise our space, even when it is temporary.

I love reading the different names listed next to the buzzers, then repeated up the stairwell. It's a great expression of how diverse many Scottish communities are. It also tells of intimate histories, of families settled and dispersed. A Czech friend of mine enjoyed showing me the old nameplate fixed next to the buzzers in a Leith tenement printed with the name of her husband's great-grandfather; many years later, she and her family lived not 200 metres away in a very similar building.

**Many people heroically use their front door space to the max** by surrounding it with thriving, trailing plants as well as storing bikes, shoes and buggies. This reflects a certain level of trust and camaraderie between neighbours and perhaps indicates further nuances in their relationships. I always find tenement closes intriguing; often the items kept outside doorways echo what many home owners without closes keep within their homes on the other side of the front door. Just like a well-used front step, open porch or garden, you can learn so much about someone from how they personalise and populate such a small space.

A friend who works as a school's outdoors coordinator keeps all his sporting equipment at his front door just as you enter his home. You are immediately met with three bikes and enough sets of skis to start a ski school. It feels like he is trying to bring the outdoors into his home and, arguably, he is succeeding!

My family home in North Berwick has an incredible, unique entranceway. As you open the front door, you enter into an architectural fusion of stone elements from a medieval abbey that once stood near to the plot. The design unites these with replica stones that finish the vestibule, creating a space with an almost spiritual calm. When the old and new meet in an interior or exterior design, it seems that the fusion emulates Scotland and creates a distinct coorie feel. This remarkable atmosphere and sense of history present in the now make draughts, leaks and the damp worth it!

" Books are integral to the feel of a house – they insulate, decorate, personalise. "

PHILIPPA COCHRANE, SCOTTISH BOOK TRUST

# Make Your Own
# No Sew Draught Excluder

**Got any old troosers lying around? Jeans nearing the end of their life are perfect for this. For smaller draught excluders, long-sleeved tops are equally as good.**

**You will need:**
tape measure
sharp scissors
old long-sleeved tops or trousers that you were going to throw away. Jeans are great to use as the fabric is nice and robust
something to stuff it with: toy or pillow stuffing, old socks, wool or packaging from delivery boxes are fab
optional: string or ribbon

**Method:**

1. Start by measuring the door you want to make the draught excluder for. You need to measure the width and depth to make sure it fits snugly (to exclude those draughts!) and so that you won't trip over it.

2. Think about the floor on which your draught excluder will sit – if it's in a 'high traffic' area it could get quite grubby. Darker fabrics are therefore ideal.

3. Cut the sleeves or legs off of your garment of choice, so they are as close to your measurements as possible.

4. From the remaining fabric cut strips that are as long as possible and ideally 2cm wide.

5. Take a leg or sleeve of fabric, and either use the strips of remaining fabric or your preferred string/ribbon and tie one end closed.

6. Stuff it with your chosen material until it is pretty firm but not too stiff or solid.

7. Then tie the other end of the draught excluder closed and squish the sausage into shape.

8. That's it – you're finished! Now you can enjoy a draught-free, coorie night in.

# Sharing's Caring

Communal living in all its forms

3

## A definition of COMMUNITY

1. A group of people living together in one place, especially one practising common ownership.
2. A group of people having a religion, race, profession or other particular characteristic in common.
3. The condition of sharing or having certain attitudes and interests in common.

*The New Oxford Dictionary of English*

## A definition of COMMUNAL

1. Shared by all members of a community; for common use.
2. Of, relating to or done by a community.

*The New Oxford Dictionary of English*

# TRIBE, CLAN AND FAMILY

The communities of Scotland are derived from the many different types of social structures the country has seen. One that enjoys an international status is the idea of the Scottish clan. The word 'clan' (from the Gaelic *clann* meaning 'offspring, family') was introduced into English in around 1425.

Since then clans have become poster boys for what we might call 'abstracted Scottishness', as it sometimes feels like there is more chat about clans internationally, in the USA for example, than there is in Scotland. Although many Scots have some idea of their clan heritage, for most it isn't a big part of their everyday life. Even so, it seems that the essence of clan life can still be found in contemporary Scotland, as Scottish society – both tribal and modern – has always had a deep-rooted need for community and togetherness.

Our needs – whether social, economic, environmental or more personal – have always shaped what collective living looks like. And today's society is no different. For example, in 2019, author Stephen Millar explored his Glaswegian roots in a photographic celebration of the city's different peoples: *Tribes of Glasgow* showcases the variety of communities, old and new, found in contemporary Glasgow. Stephen's choice of the word 'tribe' to delineate the diverse groups that make up Scotland's biggest city shows how clan living is much more than an expression of historical Scottish life. It's an idea we can still connect with in a myriad of meaningful ways.

## STRUCTURAL COMMUNAL LIVING

For me, two types of housing embody community in Scotland: the tenement and the blackhouse.

**Tenement buildings – of the kind that are so specifically Scottish – started to appear more than 400 years ago.** The need for these tenements – terraced, four-storey blocks of homes that share, except for the 'main door' flat in many buildings, a common stairwell – arose from those economical, political and topographical factors that drove people to share domestic space and facilities. Still incredibly popular as residential accommodation, the tenements of cities such as Edinburgh and Glasgow tend today not to be associated with living in poverty. Of course, different tenements enjoy varying degrees of grandeur, size, outdoor space and aesthetic appeal, but in contrast to those found beyond the UK – for example, in New York – the tenements of Scotland are uniquely comfortable.

**Blackhouses are the traditional houses of the Scottish Highlands and the Hebrides.** Encompassing all that's distinctive about life in the Highlands and Islands, black-houses are a form of the traditional long-house buildings historically built across

Europe from around 7000 BCE. With just one long room, blackhouses usually had a thatched roof, no chimney and provided a home for both livestock and people. They were the most common form of shelter in northern Scotland until the mid-18th century – although the blackhouses at Gearrannan were occupied as recently as the 1970s. Now hostel accommodation, you can stay there for an authentic blackhouse experience.

Likewise, if you visit the blackhouse in Arnol, on the Isle of Lewis, by smelling the peat fire and seeing the original furnishing in the interior, you can imagine how it would have been to live in one.

## CLANS AND BLACKHOUSES

Communities have always built homes that reflect and adapt to their surrounding environment. This is nowhere more apparent than in wild places. It is no surprise then that the remoteness, the mountains, glens and rivers, coupled with the harsh climate of northern Scotland greatly influenced the construction and subsequent growth of Highland culture and community.

For more than 500 years the (mainly Gaelic) clans of the Highlands and Islands consisted of small farming communities whose lives were lived out on fertile land. These communities

(*clachan*) were formed of a small number of families living in groupings of blackhouses and associated outbuildings. One half of the blackhouse would be used by the family for eating, sleeping and entertaining, and the other would house the family's livestock. The surrounding land – known as 'infields' – adjacent to the settlements was communal and used for cultivation. The land surrounding these infields – 'outfields' – was used for cattle grazing.

The form and spatial arrangement of the blackhouses both reflected the practical requirements for living, such as providing comfort and respite from the weather and a place to cook food, and the Gaelic cultural belief in kinship, the symbiotic relationship between the individual, the family and the community.

Kinship is perhaps best seen in the large living spaces of the blackhouses. These spaces provided a setting for social gatherings – ceilidhs, communal storytelling, singing and music, which would have typically been held around a peat fire, the heart of any blackhouse home.

Another example of the Gaelic culture of community is how people leave their front doors unlocked; this is still often done on the Islands. Having a 'wanderer's stone' was a symbolic way of welcoming strangers and would be found just inside the front door. However, the Highland

clan structure and its unique patterns of life hugely diminished in the early 18th century when Scotland signed the Union with England (1707) and indigenous ways of life were discouraged.

**The blackhouse is integral to an understanding of Scottish history, culture and way of life.** Although it was sometimes seen as a rudimentary type of home, many native Highlanders and Islanders see the blackhouse as a representation of Gaelic traditions that have been lost through centuries of colonial oppression. For a long time, the imposition of English rule and architecture overshadowed Gaelic ideals of kinship and community.

Awareness of the implications of these losses have led architectural firms such as Dualchas (meaning culture or heritage in Gaelic) to revitalise the blackhouse in contemporary architecture. At the 'forefront of a new awakening' of Scottish architecture, Dualchas was the first to create a modern longhouse, with the intention of looking to provide socially and economically deprived communities with meaningful, low-cost homes while also bolstering the growth in conversations about Scottish Highland identity.

This re-imagined blackhouse (or longhouse) is an integral part of the landscape of Scotland, in both a topographic and industrial sense. By using local materials in their raw forms, new builds, such as Dualchas's longhouse, showcase what local areas have to offer. They speak powerfully in more than one way to the local community. The structure hails pre-Union elements such as robust roofs, thick walls and east-facing doors and windows. More importantly, the longhouses value large open-plan layouts, which reflect the footprint of the ancient Highland dwellings. The connections they create with the lost homes of Scotland are transformative.

Coorie Bookshelf

## *His Bloody Project*
## Graeme Macrae Burnet

## INDUSTRIAL GROWTH AND COMMUNITY

The Industrial Revolution saw the creation of many new social and economic units, such as the unique mill village of New Lanark, as well as the expansion of existing cities such as Glasgow. New tenements were erected, and many older buildings reworked to maximise their capacity, so as to provide homes for people as their communities grew in size.

High demand for workers meant that overcrowding soon became an issue in most Scottish industrial hubs. Leasing laws in Scotland tended to favour landlords, which resulted in tenants renting smaller spaces, which in turn led to overcrowding. By 1914, Glasgow was the most densely populated urban area in Europe with no fewer than 700,000 people living within three square miles of the Glasgow Cross.[i]

The majority of Scottish families who lived in these cramped conditions were households headed by labourers or unskilled workers.[ii] The layout of tenement blocks was a key contributing factor in this overcrowding. Some early tenements – for instance, the closes of the High Street and Grassmarket districts of Edinburgh – consisted of one-room

apartments. These single rooms were reorganised twice daily to adapt to the day- and night-time needs of the residents.

On the other hand, Gladstone's Land on the High Street, bought and restored by the National Trust Scotland in 1934, is a living example of wealthy – and sometimes scandalous – tenement life in the 17th century.

The less luxurious conditions in urban tenements forced people to live literally much closer to one another, which can't have always been on the comfortable side of coorie – but, the flip side of such tight-packed housing was that its residents would also forge tight-knit communities within their tenements. For example, household budgeting decisions were not necessarily made in isolation but might be decided as a community.

Other communal elements of tenement living involved the sharing of a wide variety of utilities – toilets, water, cooking, washing and laundry facilities. Meanwhile, the high costs of supplying gas to these high-rise tenement dwellings delayed the provision of gas lighting and hot water to the residents. This meant tenement life was even more labour intensive for working-class women of the time: daily domestic tasks required frequent trips up and down the many flights of stone stairs. Today, you can see that the treads of such tenements are well worn and bevelled, a permanent reminder of all those trips made over the decades.

Women adapted to this higher workload by banding together to share childcare. The smooth running of such arrangements involved distinct social routines that reflected the needs of each family. For example, the use of the communal wash house in the back court or basement was organised on a rota basis, strict adherence to which was key to preventing arguments and rifts in the community.

The sensibility of trust, respect and good-neighbourliness is one that holds today for 21st-century tenement dwellers – as can be seen by those notices pinned by communal exits requesting everything from reminders to close the door properly to invitations to help yourself to the apples in the shared garden.

# CONTEMPORARY CO-LIVING

Today, we live in differently shared living spaces – often for longer than expected – for a number of reasons, but most commonly to save money or, to put it another way, because we simply can't afford the alternatives. Apparently, the average Scot expects to move out of their family house by the tender age of 22. In reality more than one in ten adults are still living with a parent or two at the age of 40.

The number of young adults living at home has increased steadily over the last 20 years, recently reaching a record high since 1996. The reasons for this are wide-ranging and politically contro-versial, but the sky-high cost of either renting or owning a home 'of one's own' in Scotland's most sought-after cities plays a significant role. There have been dramatic increases in deposits required for urban properties since 2008, with an average of 50% of income required in 2016. In addition, the cost of living while renting a property is becoming so expen-sive that it can be extremely difficult to save up for a deposit.

To give Scottish homes a more interna-tional perspective, the average American home is 819m$^2$ compared to the average Scottish home of 250m$^2$. This difference demonstrates the challenges that arise from shared living – there is, quite clearly, limited physical space. We can also see that more unrelated individuals, such as students and young professionals, are 'choosing' to live together from the fact that the number of licences for houses in multiple occupation (HMO) have increased year by year since 2001.

**Living with friends or strangers is not something that older generations would have necessarily done,** so we are in new territory. However, there are definite advantages to shared living based on these more fluid and less emotionally restricting relationships. Without romance involved, there is no need for the potential heartbreak that can come from being compelled to share with a romantic partner. There's more freedom that can be experienced in different shared living experiences – especially for women.

Living with others helps you save money by splitting costs, but it might also help you become a more well-rounded person. While living with family, or people who know you very well, you can rely on them understanding you through body language and the things you leave unsaid. When living with people you haven't previously known, you have to communicate more clearly, as new flatmates-cum-strangers won't know your quirks and irks, and certainly can't read your mind. You'll learn how to be friendly with people without necessarily having to be friends with them, and the ability to do this will aid you in other social and professional situations.

Coorie Bookshelf

*Tribes of Glasgow*
Stephen Millar

# Top tips for having your own space in a shared home

## Create more space

If sharing a home, you might need to set boundaries and get creative with what you have in order to create your own space to relax. A great way to do this is by using practical solutions such as bookcases that will also help you maximise space. By setting these perpendicular to a wall, you can create multiple living areas and provide much needed storage space at the same time.

## Create the ultimate coorie

When sharing a home with others who you aren't in a relationship with, you will always have that one space that is truly yours: your bed. The ultimate cosy spot deserves TLC, so be sure to invest in good sheets and pillows to make it truly a space you want to spend time in. Headboards are also a good shout as they protect your wall and your head, as well as adding an extra personal touch to the space.

## Living-room microcosms

Sharing is great, but for your sanity sometimes having your own perch is needed. Therefore, as much as sofas are perfect for saving space, finding a lovely armchair to nestle in to watch TV or read is a perfect way to have your own space in a communal area. In addition, if there is a spare corner or alcove in the home, making a wee reading nook by sourcing a comfy perch and a decent light source is another way to create a microcosm for yourself.

# CULTURE OF WELLNESS: CONTEMPORARY SCOTTISH COMMUNITIES

## CARE

Corbenic Camphill Community is four miles from the picturesque town of Dunkeld, and 20 miles from Perth. The community is part of the International Camphill Movement and, since 1978, the team at Corbenic has met the needs of adults with complex and severe disabilities by creating an integrated community.

Colum, the general manager of Corbenic, observes that the community takes a different approach to care from a lot of residential facilities. Instead of what he terms a 'bums-on-seats' method, the residents are invited to participate in more gratifying activities such as learning how to maintain gardens and small agricultural ventures. They also learn skills such as pottery and woodwork, thereby enabling them to sell products in Dunkeld at the Corbenic community shop.

With 40 employees, 30 international volunteers and 40 residents, Corbenic is far from a small community. But the informed, gentle and personal approach that the staff and volunteers provide means the people of Corbenic can forge deep connections to their neighbours as well as the wider community of Perthshire. The Corbenic community prides itself on its commitment to long-term sustainability and the love of arts and crafts that upholds its ethos. Visiting the community shop is definitely worthwhile, as is walking the Corbenic poetry path, which is always open, and includes work by over 17 poets and carving by the esteemed Martin Reilly.

## EAT

Porteous' Studio is a beautifully peaceful, nurturing residential space for short holiday stays that is nestled in the dramatic shadow of Edinburgh Castle. Tucked away in the Grassmarket, the studio is the debut project of Izat Arundell, showcasing the ethos of their design practice which encompasses Scottish architecture, craft and food. The space is also used to host a series of supper clubs for fellow designers, craftspeople and thinkers.

Jack Arundell – one half of the couple that makes up Izat Arundell – talked with me about the deep and fruitful connection he believes exists in Scotland between design and food. For their monthly supper clubs, the pair use the custom-built oak table in the studio apartment; its broad, clean lines and minimal finish effortlessly tie into the quiet tactile feeling of the studio, as the centre of the communal eating experience.

> " I believe that collective self-build developments
> such as the Findhorn Ecovillage in Scotland
> engender a greater sense of community, as
> everyone involved puts their heart and soul into
> every part of the project – not just the bricks and
> mortar, but the landscaping, public spaces and
> continuing maintenance. "

GEORGE CLARKE, *THE RESTORATION MAN* AND
*GEORGE CLARKE'S AMAZING SPACES*

## GROW

In the north of Scotland, the Findhorn Ecovillage can be found. The community first began when three individuals came to the Findhorn Bay Caravan Park near the village of Findhorn in 1962. They created a garden out of necessity that, despite the soil being extremely sandy, produced crops that amazed all who saw them. The community grew by leaps and bounds from there.

Since the 1980s, the Findhorn Ecovillage has worked to express the community's commitment to sustainability by building ecological houses using innovative materials such as local stone, straw bales and tyres, and by prioritising beauty in its architecture and gardens. As well as through the physical elements of the ecovillage, the community contributes to a sustainable future by supporting green businesses and social initiatives. The community's home and energy footprint is 22% of the UK national average – the lowest measured for any settlement in the industrialised world, according to a study by the Stockholm Environment Institute.

Miraculously, all this work was started by a handful of people, who persevered through environmental and financial limitations to create a community and ecovillage that has inspired projects internationally, and attracted 14,000 visitors from 50 countries with its centre for holistic learning.

## RESPITE

Leuchie House, located in East Lothian, is a prime example of how historic buildings are often repurposed and used in different ways to support a range of people. Currently, Leuchie House is a respite centre for people with neurological conditions. The expert 24-hour care it provides means guests and their families can enjoy short breaks from everyday life. Even though the house sits slightly outside the town of North Berwick, Leuchie is embedded in the local community, with many locals working there. It is definitely well loved – residents of nearby towns walked to Leuchie during the extreme snow of February 2018 to deliver food and to relieve staff who were stranded there.

## INNOVATE

Where do most of us spend most of our time? With plenty of exceptions, of course – for those who are retired, in education, caring for others old and young, out of work and the rare few who are free from financial constraints – we're usually at work. And unless you work from home, you're probably out and about in a workplace environment more than you are in your home. How do we bring cultural wellness – a commitment to building positive relationships and respectful interactions with people of different backgrounds – with us throughout the working day?

Such 'cultural wellness' feels like a kinder, more generous approach to networking, more suited to our 21st-century lives. It's evident that Scotland has recently become a standout example of the power of networking. Household names such as Rockstar North, Skyscanner and Brewdog all began life as start-ups bolstered through the art of contemporary networking. There are hubs of all kinds located throughout Scotland; Aberdeen, Edinburgh and Glasgow are the largest. Naturally, these fluctuate as industry, the economy and trends shift. If you are keen to get your small business off the ground, or if you would love to meet like-minded, entrepreneurial people in similar or different industries, networking is the thing to do. Don't be daunted! Business cards, self-confidence and chat at the ready . . .

**Here are some top recommendations to get you started.**

**Entrepreneurs Social Club** – an organic online community that was started by two entrepreneurs based in Scotland. Instead of going for a traditional network format, they wanted instead to create an environment where you can connect informally perhaps over a pint. ESC now hosts regular meet-ups in the capital that aim to generate an informal and exciting environment for anyone who is interested in the world of enterprise.

**Entrepreneurial Scotland** – a mentoring, interns and business network. They facilitate meet-ups all across Scotland, as well as running Saltire programmes that aim to develop the skills and networks of early- to mid-career individuals.

**Scottish Contemporary Art Network** – a member-led network which connects and unites Scots working within the visual arts. They have initiated projects such as the 'Mandate' scheme that gives financial aid to professionals looking to attend events in the visual arts that they couldn't normally afford.

**Start-up Summit** – recognised as one of the UK's leading events for entrepreneurship. At the 2017 summit, Nicola Sturgeon called Scotland the 'home of innovation'.

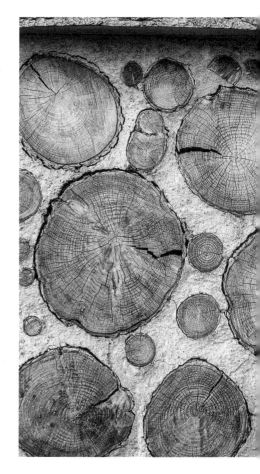

# A Holistic Approach: Cranhill Development Trust
## a case study

It goes without saying that community looks different in different places. Historically, certain urban areas carried challenges for communities. This is still the case in contemporary Scotland – there are socio-economic factors that mean living in certain areas can be harder than in others. The term 'the Glasgow effect' was created to describe these issues when they were seen as anomalies, although we have since discovered why parts of Glasgow have been hit harder than other areas of the UK. A complex combination of historical factors, political processes and decisions have resulted in areas in the East End of Glasgow having the lowest life expectancies in Britain. It can be argued that when areas are affected by such issues, community is more important then ever, becoming essential rather than optional. Parts of Glasgow living this out include Cranhill, an area developed in the 1950s that has been served by the Cranhill Development Trust (CDT) since 2002.

The Trust responds to the specific needs of the community, and as they develop and change, so do the services CDT provides. These include different kids clubs and childcare throughout the week, support for asylum seekers and refugees, jobsearch and other IT-based drop-ins, the community café, the 'nearly' new shop that sells second-hand goods.

A recent hit has been the opening of the 'Cranhill Cabin', a wee shop situated on the grounds of the CDT. The community shop, which addresses food inequality, encourages healthy eating and good stewardship of the environment, is described as an oasis in a 'food desert' as supermarkets are a bus ride away for most people. Run by volunteers and open five days a week, it sells a wide range of reasonably priced household essentials including fresh fruit and vegetables, herbs and spices.

Linda Drummond of nearby Riddrie was recently made redundant from the place where she'd worked for 27 years. She said:

> It is great to be able to buy little quantities of things which take the pressure off families on a tight budget. By the time you pay your bills, what you have left at the end of the day is not much. So knowing that you can go into this wee shop and buy a small amount of something to last you until the end of the week is great.

Maureen Moffat, the community shop manager, said:

> Things are going well, the shop is proving popular with the community and by Friday we usually have very little fruit and veg left. We sell a lot of single toilet rolls, kitchen rolls and nappies because a lot of people round here are on Universal Credit and get to the end of the month and do not have a lot of money.[iii]

## WELCOME

Globally, the number of people seeking refuge is on the rise, driven in large part by conflict and political instability across the world.

If we are to live in a diverse, inclusive Scotland where we all have the opportunity to achieve our potential, it is everyone's responsibility to welcome 'New Scots', and to connect and collaborate with one another. Fantastic organisations such as the Scottish Refugee Council and innovative charities such as The Welcoming help make this possible.

The Welcoming enables newcomers to Edinburgh to feel at home and connect with life in Scotland. It offers practical support along with activities ranging from reading groups to sustainable gardening workshops, from digital skills to language classes. With its amazing team of volunteers, at the heart of The Welcoming's work is a befriending programme that develops social and cultural bonds.

## Community Meal

Research has revealed that the more we eat together, the more likely we are to feel satisfied, joy-filled and connected to those around us. This can only bode well for communities that break bread on a regular basis. People who eat socially are more likely to feel better about themselves and have a wider social network capable of providing social and emotional support.[iv] Eating together is integral to many communities and can be really helpful to those who take part in intense physical or social activities together. For example, Edinburgh-based community outreach group Streetlights meet weekly to eat together before going out to provide support to sex workers in the city. They swear by a timeless classic: the baked potato, but this low-cost, high-satisfaction meal is great for any community occasion.

**You will need:**

1 medium-large potato per person
1 or 2 toppings per person to share. Try:
  something from your garden such as salad
  leaves or roasted root veg
  baked beans
  cheese or a dairy-free alternative
  steamed kale
  for crunchy protein, roast some chickpeas
  with parmesan and garlic
  coronation chicken
  tuna mayonnaise

**Method:**

1. Clean and then prick each potato with a fork, rub with olive oil, salt and pepper, and then bake in the oven at 220°C for about 1 hour 20 minutes.
2. Add toppings, serve and enjoy.
3. Don't forget to give a prize for the most out-there topping!

# That's a Bit Naff

## The unfolding of Scottish interiors

## 4

At the heart of coorie is the idea of cosying up with nature. Ancient Scottish ways of living relied on the land to shape homes, and this still prevails today – whether your dwelling is a new-build made with bright and distinctive sandstone or you live in a remote part of the Highlands where your home is literally etched into a cliff.

Interiors are no different! You can't live in Scotland, however much you are inside, without being affected by nature – and by the weather. Historically, people have combated the seasonal depression that affects so many of us by creating internal sanctuaries that acknowledge the howling gales, long days of dreich and darkness, and muffling snowfall that exist outside but that also exude light and life, warmth and colour on the inside. Balancing the contrasts between light and dark in the home feels essential to our wellbeing in so many ways.

# THE INFLUENCE OF THE OUTSIDE

The Scottish Vernacular Buildings Group has defined historical Scottish buildings such as the blackhouse as 'integrated structures within the landscape ... [whose] form, shape and colour merged naturally with the fields'.

The external structure, interior space and site orientation of blackhouses were all developed to minimise the impact of the windy and wet Highland environment on its residents and to create a warm, protective refuge in landscapes that offered none.

In crofting communities, the early 20th-century blackhouses evolved with only slight differences from the homes that marked their historic origins. Interior improvements – such as planked wooden flooring and wall panelling, glazed windows, mass-produced imported furniture – were all made. A significant, life-changing adjustment – one that offered an enclosed, repositioned source of heat and comfort – was the replacement of the central hearth with gable-end hearths, which would often be fitted with cast-iron stoves.[i]

## TARTAN AND TAXIDERMY

In recent centuries, the British upper classes have perceived – and used – the Highlands as a playground that offers ample opportunities for hunting and other 'country sports'. Most famously, ever since her first visit in 1842, Queen Victoria became renowned for her love for the country. And when, in the 19th century, the antlers of the red deer became a symbol of Scotland, hunting trophies became an obvious source of decorative ideas inside Scottish homes, beginning perhaps with the most wealthy and grand.

Hunting lodges have a distinctive style of their own, with some of the early Scottish lodges almost seeming to grow out of the landscape that surrounds them. They are horizontally planned with entrances taking the shape of porticoes and verandas crafted from raw tree trunks. With their commanding views of lochs, mountains and glens, and snug patterns of tartan carpets within, they offer a particular, privileged interpretation of the 'authentic Scottish hut'.

The outside of these huts feels bold and baronial, but still they seem to fit well with the wild grandeur of the Scottish landscape. Inside, however, these references feel more problematic – they speak of a take on history and a culture that many Scots find unnerving. The

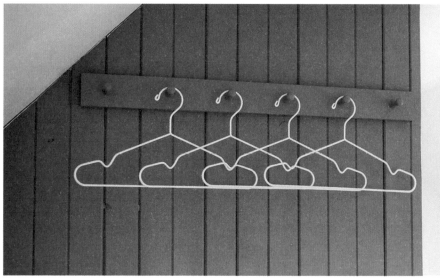

presence of the external world is sublime, but the inhabitants looking out at it exist in something of a stage-set – it's a style replete with theatrical and opulent overtones, which gives rise to a pastiche of Scottish identity. The hunting lodge, in its tendency towards what has become an international stereotype of how Scotland looks, treads close to being sham, while at the same time distorting contemporary ideas of nationhood and independence.

## INTERNATIONAL INFLUENCES

Arguably, Scotland has always been an international country. Archaeological evidence suggests that, as far back as 500 BCE, Scots have traded across Europe. Evidence of this can be found in the botanical remains at Loch Tay where spelt has been found – a crop that originally would have grown in Eastern Europe. There is evidence to suggest that even 500 years before the written word as we know it was present, Highland dwellers were carving huge log boats and trading as far as the Netherlands.

The Scottish Enlightenment in the 18th and 19th centuries saw the renewal of Scottish art, literature and philosophy. The wide-ranging, international reach of Scotland – and the exchange of ideas during the enlightenment period – is reflected in Scottish architecture, culture and ideas. Whether it's an unfinished facsimile of the Parthenon looming atop Edinburgh's Calton Hill, the Japanese garden at Cowden Castle or the diverse range of plants in the Royal Botanical Gardens in both Edinburgh and Glasgow.

The Scottish assemblage of other cultures, which fused with the upper-class influence through the popularity of hunting, in terms of its motifs and aesthetic, generated an eclectic style. At the grandest level, this can be seen in stately

Coorie Bookshelf

*Made in Scotland*
Billy Connolly

homes across Scotland, where taxidermy and 'exotic' artefacts alike have been passed down through generations. There are positives and negatives at play here: a colonial past isn't something to be celebrated, but neither should it be ignored. On the flip side, visionary creatives such as Charles Rennie Mackintosh – and his 'genius' wife Margaret Macdonald Mackintosh – introduced more European stylistic influences to the domestic and cultural lives of middle- and working-class homes, helping to introduce international influences on a wider scale.

## INTENTIONALITY

However, it does need to be said that Scottish homes haven't always been blessed with what one might call 'good taste'. Indeed, my experience is of some truly questionable interiors. I can't be the only person who can still picture the swirls of my grandparents' brown and orange carpet in my mind's eye.

But more seriously, I feel that all the various design eras are reflected, for better or for worse, in our contemporary Scottish homes. The ethos of staying warm, dry and cosy, and of making the most of what is around you, is very much present. So is the love of tweed and tartan, and the symbol of the red deer. The presence of game in the home is now, thank goodness, more in the form of fabric wall mounts with majestic faux antlers, prints and cushions – not actual stuffed animals.

These elements culminate in a fresh Scottish take that's more minimalist, ironic and playful than opulent and regal in its acknowledgement of the old and welcoming of the new.

Indeed, archaeological evidence shows how seeking out, creating and displaying items that are imbued with sentimental value is an age-old tradition in Scotland.

For example, a shelving feature exists in a Neolithic farmstead at the Knap of Howar, on the island of Papa Westray in Orkney. Archaeologists have suggested that this aspect of the dwelling serves a similar purpose to that of a mantelpiece or windowsill in a contemporary home. And, as such, it would have held items of personal significance. If this is the case, then the Neolithic farmers might well have regarded those items with a similar reverence, fondness and attachment that a modern resident feels for the prized sculptures, inherited pieces, *objets trouvés* and keepsakes – the knick-knacks of my grandparents' generation – that our 'storage solutions' display today.

**Maggie Tome, a budding Edinburgh-based interior designer, met me at the beautifully renovated Eden Locke Hotel, in their third-wave café, 127.**

Maggie describes interior design as her playground and sees minimalism in Scottish interior design as a collection of considered choices, ones that work through the psychology of cleanliness and intentionality. This is quite different to the international minimalism move-ment, which champions stark spaces,

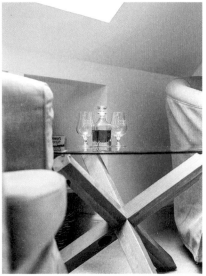

as Scottish minimal interiors are not empty-looking. In our conversation, we agreed that, as the Scottish seasons are extremely interchangeable and easily defined, interiors need to be uniquely adaptable to different temperatures and levels of light. Layering textures and furniture pieces helps to create this flexible atmosphere. The beauty of layering is also helpful if you have furniture that is a little the worse for wear, as you can revamp it with blankets, throws, rugs and cushions if you can't afford to start afresh. In that sense, Scottish minimalism brings a feeling of economic freedom as, by making wise decisions around furniture and other key pieces wisely, you may well spend less in the long run.

Coorie Bookshelf

*The Scottish Nation*
Tom Devine

# LIGHT

Keeping the majority of walls in your home white or in bright, clear shades enhances daylight, even if there is very little of it. This is especially important in flats or semi-detached homes that have windows facing in just one or two directions. A compass is your friend when choosing a home – a north-facing property can feel immeasurably bleaker and colder than those with a westerly or southerly aspect.

Charles Rennie Mackintosh certainly knew this: he drew attention to the significance of south- and north-facing windows through his work. As a trained artist with an exceptional reputation, he knew – instinctively and through experience – the value of different kinds of light. If there are structural elements in a home, such as beams supporting the roof, painting these white can alleviate darkness and open up the space. Statement walls can help break up a space, too. These have become so popular that new-builds and renovations of historical buildings for residential use across Scotland are often styled to include faux brick or rough stone statement walls; these are there for their aesthetic qualities – they have no actual structural value at all!

# ARCHITECTURAL EMBROIDERY

**Cornices and other decorative mouldings were introduced to Britain from the Roman Empire in the 1st century AD.**
Much later, when Scots emigrated to the Americas, they took the concept of cornicing with them. As a decorative style, cornicing can tell you a lot about the importance and function of a room. A heavily decorated ceiling is an expensive, complex undertaking. A room with intricate and elaborate cornicing would be used for entertaining, so as to display this show of wealth and status to others.

Architectural embroidery such as moulding has been lost in some historical homes, but, where it has survived, I feel it champions Scotland's inherent creativity and love of detail. If your Scottish home has cornicing or moulding then be sure to enjoy it – and to keep an eye out for it in other places such as cafés, workplaces and public buildings. If the plasterwork in your home is in need of restoration, and you can afford it, then it really is well worth repairing – if only because it makes such a pleasing, beautiful addition to your living space.

Many Scottish homes do not have a problem when it comes to high ceilings and big windows (quite the opposite, in fact), but if you want to make a room feel bigger, then painting or decorating the ceiling is the way to go.

Making sure your walls and floors are light in colour also helps create an expansive feeling of space. If your home feels too cavernous and you struggle to create a cosy, warm interior, try opting for a more earthy palette with pops of colour and see whether these visual tricks allow your space to feel more homely.

A simple way to incorporate colour into a room without embarking on a large-scale painting project is to paint architraves, the frames around doors or windows. Earthy tones can reflect the home's connection to nature, whereas bright pastels or fuller, more daring colours can add a contemporary spin to a historical interior. Dividing a room with different textures, light fittings or colours can help to designate particular spaces for different tasks. Bringing a focused sense of intentionality to these will help you create a united, coherent interior with cosiness spread throughout.

## FORM OF FUNCTIONALITY

With our collective realisation that to combat climate change we need to reconsider our lifestyles, it is more relevant than ever to meditate on how our homes affect nature.

Interestingly, in the 1990s, Scotland was considered a very environmentally unfriendly country, and in the same decade had much higher rates of illness than other countries in Northern Europe. So, not only is being conscious of sustainability important in your interior-design choices for the outside world, it can also be argued that it's crucial for our individual and collective wellbeing too.

**Home can be a central part of your identity, so it makes sense to create spaces for your specific needs.** The 'flow' of a room, while admittedly a phrase that is sometimes overused, is significant. What are the intentioned activities for each room?

Consider the kitchen, for example. The kitchen can often be the most vital room in the house. It is a natural place to congregate, to make food, to chat over a shared activity and to eat together. Often homes will have a designated area, such as a lounge or a living room, for hosting, yet as everyone knows, at any social gathering you are likely to find everyone congregated happily in the kitchen instead. Unless, of course, they have specifically been told not to!

**It used to be that the fireplace offered a focal point for a living room.** But, with the onset of central heating, the need for a fireplace decreased and furniture is now often arranged to reflect the position of televisions and other electronic devices. However, there is a very strong trend for the fire to form the heart of the home once more; log-burning stoves are enjoying a huge resurgence in popularity.

Perhaps when planning a space, you could reinstate a fireplace or mantelpiece as the main focus of the room – bringing back the cosy, coorie element of the Scottish home that has been essential for centuries. If not, features such as shelving with inbuilt TVs have provided a great solution to this creative issue by not banishing the TV altogether but using shape and colour to draw the eye to other elements in the room.

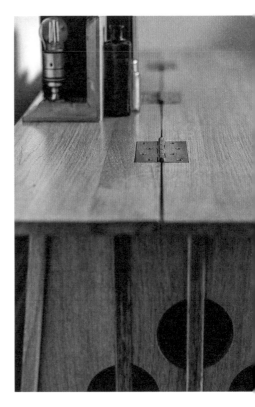

# International Inverness
## a case study

The Highlands have always expressed a strong sense of the value of community, and are known for their genuinely warm welcome. But still people can find integration into Highland society tricky if they haven't always lived there. Groups based in and around Inverness work hard to help recent new arrivals, particularly refugees, feel at home in northern Scotland.

I went to Inverness to meet a family of non-native Highlanders, with strong ties to the Middle East, who have blazed a trail at welcoming 'New Scots' to the local community. They welcomed me warmly into their beautiful, plant-filled home, which had once been an outbuilding for a farm, or possibly an 'ecurie' (another contender for the origins of the word 'coorie'). The interior reflected in its style and ornamentation the diversity of communities and cultures the family had been part of before moving to Inverness.

As I saw it, the family championed the values that stand at the forefront of Highland culture: sustainability and community. Though they encountered their own difficulties in terms of integrating into the Highland community, they strove to create their own community too, through gardening, growing produce and craft work. At their community events, you will find people from many different backgrounds enjoying a vast array of tea and delicious snacks as their children mingle and run wild and happy in the garden.

# Inverness upcycling

The family told me that the majority of the furniture in their home was discovered at local flea markets and scrapyards. A fine collection was also liberated from skips and, in the case of one gleaming glass cabinet, taken straight from the street. I admired their style! It's a great lesson in true sustainability. If a piece is sound of structure, easy to sand, paint and varnish – then why not consider making it good for its new home: yours! Just remember to reinforce any shelves if you are planning to stack crockery or tinned goods on them.

# SCOTTISH INTERIOR DESIGN
## A ROUND-UP

With the help of Platform 9 International, a Glasgow-based interior design practice, here are some significant points to take away on the ethos and aesthetic of contemporary Scottish interior design.

### What are the key looks in Scottish interior design at the moment?

Scotland continues to value style over trend. This is why elements of ancient Scottish homes remain present today. Original features are highlighted and restored for both functional and aesthetic effect. You can witness the use of natural fibres to warm the home, such as natural fibre-based insulation, furs and woollen blankets, and fires. Trends come and go, but Scottish style is knowledge-based and shows timeless taste and refinement.

Interiors within traditional listed buildings are modernised with careful consideration to the original proportions and period features. Traditional heritage is still prominent throughout Scottish interiors, designers continue to use high-quality local craftsmanship, artists and textile designers.

Peter Holmes, a remarkably passionate upholsterer who runs the furniture company Be Seated in Leith, Edinburgh, reminisced that, in previous centuries, Britain seemed to have it all: as a country it was the world's leading manufacturer of furniture. However, now that those trades have boomed internationally, the creative specs now available in Scotland have the opportunity to become much more bespoke. This doesn't mean the talent or knowledge has been lost. Furniture makers nationally and internationally, post-Bauhaus, tend to draw their inspiration from historical manufacturers. This means that the techniques and style typical of the British Isles are very much alive and well.

Craftspeople, such as Eoghann of Eoghann Menzies Design, take delight in and inspiration from the Arts and Crafts movement and apply this to handmade furniture and functional art that embody Scottish heritage while being unmistakably modern. The originality of these carefully considered, joyful Mackintosh-esque

creations lends itself well to the idea of a home that nods both to the future and to the past.

People have always been very resourceful in Scotland. And you can follow in that fine tradition. Challenging yourself to reupholster a key piece that has been in the family for generations, or that you have stumbled across in a junk shop – or even reclaimed from the roadside – is a great way to create a completely unique interior as well as showing a commitment to the joys and benefits of upcycling. Any moderately tough and durable fabric, and I mean any, can be used to reupholster a piece of furniture. From a family tartan – or a charity-shop kilt – to an old pair of jeans or two.

**How has Scottish interior design developed over the years?**
Collaborations with Scottish artists and designers continue to translate the traditional Scottish style into modern design. For example, Andrew Muirhead of Glasgow is highly respected in the leather industry and is the only specialist in the world to hold the Low Carbon Leather logo. His work is featured in many well-established hotels as well as on Peter Holmes's pieces for Be Seated.

Iconic traditional tartan is still very much present throughout Scottish interiors – especially as soft furnishings with a hint of irony in ornamentation. Many of the patterns and styles of tartan have developed over the years through shifts in colour, pattern and texture.

People are now able to travel globally and take inspiration from other countries and cultures, bringing these influences home to incorporate into their living spaces. Scottish interiors have embraced this mixed palette to keep up with people's expectations; however, we are confident they will always retain that distinctive Scottish charm.

**How might you make a home more coorie?**
Given that Scotland can experience 'all four seasons in one day' . . . it's important to consider lighting, texture and colour when designing your Scottish home.

Use textiles with a density of texture to create a layering effect, which can be utilised in different ways depending on the season. Traditional Harris Tweed is a luxury option which looks beautiful and conserves heat brilliantly. It can be pricey, so keep a lookout for high-quality Scottish wool alternatives such as woollen mix products and recycled wools which are available from the Tartan Blanket Co. Most of their visually stunning and super-snug recycled blankets are made with a combination of wool and material from old clothing and other products that would otherwise end up in landfill.

It's important to introduce character and charm throughout the home using artwork, accessories and meaningful pieces. David Cass is a Scottish artist whose work complements Scottish interiors while showcasing the sea that surrounds. Cass creates atmospheric, haunting three-dimensional paintings using exclusively found objects and surfaces sourced

at flea markets around Scotland and Europe, though his practice also involves photography, digital media and sculpture.

Scents and light are essential. From traditional fires such as those found in the ancient crannogs of Scotland, to the scents provided by handmade candles and diffusers.

To make your home uniquely yours, a living space that you can truly connect with and be nourished, calmed and invigorated by, you can showcase items – whether they be books, artworks, *objets trouvés*, childhood mementos and photographs – in the home that evoke memory and emotion.

**How do Scottish interiors reflect the Scottish landscape?**
Artists and designers continue to derive inspiration from the beautiful diversity of the Scottish landscape. We see emerging designers translate the Scottish landscape artistically into textiles, wallcoverings and artwork. Toshie Mackintosh is a prime example of a fantastic reinterpretation of classic Scottish visuals. Their designs are centred around the 'Toshie

Nine Square' brand and are evocative of the 'Master's' geometric tile motifs which, among other influences, drew upon the simplicity of Japanese art and are to be found in many of Charles Rennie Mackintosh's designs. Another glorious facet to the collection is the 'Mackintosh Tartan', handwoven exclusively in Harris Tweed from the Outer Hebrides.

It is remarkable to see how new homes in particular use the outdoor landscape as their natural colour scheme. Designing your home with floor-to-ceiling windows creates a frame for the views beyond, bringing the outdoors inside like an ever-changing piece of artwork.

**Where do you see Scottish interior design going in the future?**
I believe Scotland will continue to keep up with the demands of the international interior market while always retaining the Scottish charm! Creative collaborations within the Scottish design industry will ensure that Scotland continues to produce unique interiors with a genuinely wide-ranging appeal both here and further afield.

# Aw That Clutter

Decorating your home

## 5

After structural elements of the home are sorted, thinking about decorating your space could well take up a lot of time and energy. But it doesn't have to break the bank, nor do you have to conform to the trends of the high street. A touch of Scottish resourcefulness can alleviate the stresses of homemaking and allow for really unique interiors.

## GETTING DRESSED

So, you've sussed out the other elements of your home, and now you're going to want to dress it to make it feel more personal. Some homes, thanks to their nature as repurposed buildings, are so unique in shape and size that finding decent furniture that works in situ can be something of a hassle. It can also be a headache trying to find products that feel individualised to your particular tastes and needs. The great thing is, to help you with all of this, there's a growing number of makers who provide high-quality crafts that reflect both sustainable values and Scotland's contemporary identity.

Tucked away in Leith, Edinburgh, next to the iconic Easter Road stadium, home to Hibernian FC, is the Albion Business Centre. Once the Dunbar lemonade factory, built in 1911, the site is now home to a variety of different businesses. You can still see the block capitals of the factory's original purpose in the redbrick of its walls. And this impressive 'ghost signwriting', along with the building's wrought-iron details and the remains of the stables nearby, give the centre an industrial-style backdrop, reflecting the diversity of the creative community that thrives there.

# 56 North
## a case study

The fantastic 56 North, designers and creators of bespoke kitchens, work out of unit 8 of the Albion Business Centre. The company passionately believes that the kitchen is the most important room in the house – as the embodiment of coorie, it is at the heart of any Scottish home.

In their work, 56 North have noticed how more open-plan living situations, such as lofts or converted barns – which have become increasingly popular over the last few decades – have emphasised the vital role aesthetics play in the kitchen. Kitchens still need to retain their purpose and coorie element, but now that they are often on display to the rest of the house, the need to showcase a more beautiful, pleasing kitchen design has increased.

With their furniture-making backgrounds, the team at 56 North apply a high level of craftsmanship to create exclusive, individually tailored kitchens that enhance the structure of the rooms and houses in which they exist. From saman wood to plywood, 56 North cater to a range of styles and prices. Richard, a key member of the team, spoke avidly about the challenges and rewards of their projects.

'We sourced and worked with wood imported from Trinidad for a kitchen in Learmonth to create a truly unique look. In contrast, we often work in partnership with ventures such as Hebhomes, which provides eco-friendly kit or "flat-packed" houses that are delivered, erected and built on request.'

**In the last hundred years, Scotland has
been challenged design-wise.** In the
early 20th century, original furniture
design tended to be only accessible for a
high-end buyer, whereas most folk generally favoured value and longevity over
furniture with a bolder style aesthetic.
When new furniture started to become
more widely accessible in the mid-1900s,
Scottish suppliers of affordable furniture
were influenced by the commercial realities of the day. Furniture, therefore, in the
post-war era was made in a more modern

style with honest uses of materials, minimalist compositions, natural forms and choice of timbers. This made perfect sense to distributors in Scotland.

The more contemporary styles spelled quality as much as any antique or reproduction piece did, and it was for this reason that Scottish makers such as Morris & Company began to rapidly accommodate the forward-thinking formulas of the Nordic school. In the last 20 years, with most furniture now sourced from overseas, Scottish furniture has re-emerged style-wise, so that many bespoke pieces now highlight elements of traditional and modern design in the creation of excellent furniture.

But of course, for many people, bespoke pieces simply are not an option because of the cost involved in designing and creating them – not to mention the sense of confidence and style awareness that can be required to commission such pieces.

**Namon Gaston, a furniture designer and maker based in Midlothian**, offers a bespoke design service and a collection of his creations to meet the needs of different markets. From unique tables to elegant chairs, his work evokes the essence of contemporary design as well as being subtly timeless. In its nod to minimalism, it embodies the clean lines and refined understatement of Northern European design. In conversation with Namon, he told me that his rural location greatly enhances the Scottish aspect of his practice, although he loves working in the more urban surroundings of Edinburgh as well.

---

**UPCYCLE** / ˈʌpsʌɪk(ə)l/
**verb** [with object]
**gerund or present participle: upcycling**

1. reuse (discarded objects or material) in such a way as to create a product of higher quality or value than the original.
2. e.g. 'the opportunity to upcycle trash, or turn it into new products, was vast'

ORIGIN 1990s: blend of up- and recycle.

---

## UPCYCLING

'Upcycling' is a term coined in 1999 by Gunter Pauli, who is known as the 'Steve Jobs or Che Guevara of sustainability'. A key aspect of sustainability is the transforming of by-products, waste materials, goods that are no longer wanted or used into new – and useful – products.

For me, this term feels so in line with the Scottish determination to make the most of whatever you have in hard times. It's an old-school, working-class philosophy that will be familiar to those outwith these borders, too. My gran was always fond of presenting me with a mountain of containers, magazines and materials, saying, 'I thought you could use these for something.' It's an approach friends tell me is encouraged in primary schools with the fabulously named 'junk modelling' projects their children do. In the coorie home, a great example of this is how you can repurpose a beautiful whisky or gin bottle to create a striking bedside lamp – or simply an impromptu vase for a sprig of delicate flowers.

## AS SOUND AS A BELL

Take the way many owners of historical buildings keep original, or simply old, features on display in their homes – such as sprung bells. These bells were usually found in stairwells, outside servants' quarters and sometimes inside servants' rooms. Each bell hung from a coiled spring so that a weight – also suspended from the spring – would continue to move even after the bell had stopped ringing. This way, servants had time to move from the service areas to the bell system to see where they were required. Electric bells became popular in the late 1800s and were formed with indicator boards: shallow, glass-fronted cases, displaying a number of small, named apertures.

Now, surrounded by contemporary furnishings and modern technology, you might glimpse the mechanics of these historical systems. Once solely present for practical use, now they make for the decorative elements of a home that speaks of the past.

## WATER WATER EVERYWHERE

With an estimated 31,460 lochs and a mainland coastline over 6,000 miles long, it is rare to be far from the sea or a body of water in Scotland. Lochs can offer us so much insight into Scotland's history through the study of underwater archaeology and the communities that have grown up around lochs. Nowadays the unspoken rule is that the exterior walls of homes in the Highlands and Islands are painted white or light coloured. Lochside homes naturally reflect the glassy surface of the water and that inspiration often continues within the home.

## BEACHCOMBING

If you fancy a super-cheap day out that's restorative and a source of thrifty treats for your coorie home, then the time-honoured tradition of beachcombing is just the ticket. It's an activity everyone can enjoy, and is so accessible and rewarding. The treasures you come across can be transformative, bringing joy and meaning into your living spaces. Just like our ancestors who collected meaningful bits and pieces for domestic display, sometimes the most valuable decorative elements of a home can be those that didn't cost a penny. Shop-bought crystals and precious stones might give instant

gratification, but they won't necessarily deliver the same satisfaction – and inter-connected memories – that finding your own sea-smoothed stones, fossils and shells, then polishing or painting them for your home, or as gifts for friends and family, will.

As you scan the beach or loch shore, stones can catch your eye with a hint of colour, distinctive texture or an interest-ing shape. And those elusive pebbles with a hole through the middle give the same rare delight as diamonds to the committed beachcomber!

Rough and polished stone are key players in Scottish architecture – from crofting communities to stone-built estates and castles. Large polished or unpolished stones can serve as book-ends, doorstops or paperweights, as well as simple organic decorative features. This is another fantastic way to bring the outside in, using local materials to enhance your home.

Stones, shells and driftwood can also add pleasure and a hint of Scotland's beaches and lochs to your garden spaces – in a little rockery with sea grasses, for example. I like to think of my beachcombing finds as everlasting bouquets of flowers – natural, unique, full of texture and colour, with the added

advantage that they won't die on you. If you are travelling around Scotland, taking a wee treasure from the sea or loch shore can be a great alternative to buying a gift from a gift shop. But please respect any restrictions on beachcombing that are indicated.

Another beautiful thing you can find on Scottish beaches are fragments of ceramics, glass and pottery that have been smoothed by the sea. Often these will still have legible patterns, slogans and branding that might show you a glimpse of their history. Store your finds in an old Kilner jar or press them into plaster of Paris to create a 3D artwork.

**Sea glass is my favourite thing to find on the beach** – I love to spot it glinting on the sand. It's perfect for bringing character and colour to any mantel. Because the sea has smoothed and sanded it naturally, it's safe to collect. There is nothing quite like a full jar of sea glass that, when placed near a window, catches the light and almost glows, pouring greeny-blue light into a room. You can frame pieces of sea glass, make earrings or other jewellery from it, create mini-cairns to stand as ornaments on shelves . . .

Another way to use sea glass is to make tealight holders out of it. An easy way to do this is by bonding the pieces

Coorie Bookshelf

*The Cone Gatherers*
Robin Jenkins

together with a decorating adhesive or superglue from your local ironmonger's or hardware store. Alternatively, take an existing plain glass jar and decorate it with your pieces of sea glass. Try etching into the pieces with a sharp tool such as a nail to personalise your design.

**Driftwood is a landmark feature of Scottish design and crafts** as, again, the sea puts its mark on the material before it finds itself washed up. The rustic look of driftwood can be beautiful as frames for mirrors and artwork, for shelving and as furniture. A strongly shaped piece can look stunning in your garden. If you're not feeling squeamish, the stripped-clean look of the skulls and bones from small birds and animals (found on a countryside walk, say) can bring definite, bold character to a room and nod to the gamekeeping and fishing histories of Scotland. It goes without saying, but please never take birds' eggs as a 'trophy' or ornament.

**Precious stones, gems and metals** are also found in Scotland – although they aren't as commonly seen or readily scavenged as other beachcombing finds! If you're a fan of geology and fossils, then Eathie Beach on the Black Isle is the place to go. This beach, made famous by the geologist Hugh Miller, who lived close by in Cromarty, is a Site of

Special Scientific Interest and if you're lucky – and eagle-eyed – you might find ammonites, fossilised mussel shells and fish scales at low tide. Again, be respectful. It's a glorious, almost magical place, perfect for birdwatching and dolphin spotting, too.

**Stinky Bay, Benbecula has long been a top spot for finding all kinds of booty.** It faces the wild expanse of the Atlantic, so fierce storms regularly deposit items swept in all the way from Canada and the USA. Take your binoculars, as it's renowned for its rare birds such as curlews and plovers.

Old or young, if you walk the beaches of Scotland long enough you will find some sort of treasure, whether permanent or to be stored in your memories. Don't forget a camera – your own shots of windswept beaches and rugged shorelines can make for standout evocative artwork in your coorie home.

# SECOND-HAND SAVIOURS

Decorating can be daunting – not least of all on a budget. You ideally want your furniture and decorating materials to be from ethical sources, strong and fit for purpose so that they won't look tired or break on you immediately.

To create a space that is comfortable, eclectic and inviting can be hard work when you're on a tight budget. But in lots of ways financial restrictions can lead to more freedom in terms of imagination, resourcefulness and sustainability. The feel-good factor is also high – there's the thrill of snapping up a bargain, meeting new people and sharing and bartering in an exchange of goods and services. A friend of mine still tells the story, a decade later, of the two antique brass light fittings she gave away from her house – and the sheer joy on the face of the woman who collected them on her bicycle. Later she sent my friend a photo of the lights polished and fabulous in situ in her hallway.

Second-hand items can come to the rescue on so many fronts. Online marketplaces have made it easy to acquire second-hand goods that are often as good as new, if not better. I really love the local giveaway culture that flourishes where you can genuinely donate to – and receive from – others in your neighbourhood. Beyond the online, there is

something truly special about rummaging through charity shops and second-hand stores in search of items with which to enhance your home.

**In Edinburgh** you can source fantastic goods in different areas. The charity shops of Stockbridge and Morningside are ace for high-end products, thanks to a well-heeled demographic. Leith Walk is one of a kind when it comes to second-hand goods. From vintage stores and auction houses, to repaired pieces in the Remakery, you might well find you don't need to go anywhere else. Explore your local area and see what you discover!

**Glasgow** offers an even vaster treasure trove of second-hand saviours.

Dumbarton Road is the mecca of West End charity shops, with the Salvation Army warehouse, the Emmaus Partick shop and many more. The Emmaus community in Glasgow opened in 2006 and now offers a home to 27 former homeless men and women, known as companions, and a recycling/reuse business with three charity shops.

Another Glasgow beauty is Retrovintage, in up-and-coming Finnieston. Retrovintage specialises in mid-century, Danish and retro vintage furniture. It's not exactly cheap, but its stunning tables, chairs and units are well worth saving up for if you're on the lookout for a breathtaking piece to make a statement with.

Hands down, the most experimental second-hand shop in the West End has to be Relics, just off of Byres Road. Whenever I go in, it's like they've just cleared out the attic of every eccentric in Scotland and shoved everything into this tiny wee shop. I've found some absolute belters here: G-plan furniture, Whitefriars vases, pretty sets of china and some old travelling trunks – all purchased for a song. Stuck for gift ideas? Want something to make your house feel a little more like a coorie home? Desperate to land a vintage toothpick holder? Then Relics is the shop for you.

Even better, the guys who run Relics add as much magic to the experience as the strange layout (if you can call 'stuff balanced on other stuff' a layout). Not to mention the cat, who pads around on top of countless antiques yet never seems to break anything. If you ask nicely enough, the owners will deliver your bigger vintage finds to a local address free of charge. That leaves you enough arm-space to carry home all the knick-knacks you absolutely couldn't leave behind. The shop has its winning formula nailed – something so seemingly chaotic shouldn't work, but it does.

# POTTERING AROUND

Ceramics have long been present in the Scottish home: decorative and functional, they are extremely versatile. If you start your morning with coffee – and possibly porridge, or toast and marmalade – then you'll have started with ceramics. And the chances are they'll dominate your day thereafter, too. Inside your brick, cement and glass home, perhaps you woke to the quartz clock, cleaned your teeth at your ceramic sink, breakfasted on pottery cups and bowls. Maybe you worked all day at a computer (packed with ceramic-based electronic components, like microchips,

capacitors or resistors), went for a swim at your local Victorian-tiled baths, before heading back home for a glass of wine, gobbling down dinner from those same pottery plates, then a relax in front of the liquid-crystal TV (or Gorilla glass smartphone), before heading for bed and setting the quartz clock, ready to rinse and repeat again tomorrow. It might not seem immediately obvious, but we do in fact live in a ceramic world, just as people have for thousands of years.

Some of the best contemporary Scottish ceramic work really amplifies a feeling of community and sustainability – whether it be a handmade collection of

mugs perfect for tea and a chat between flatmates, or ceramic vases and planters that offer a decorative way to enhance the presence of plants in the home.

Many find that working with ceramics offers a uniquely hands-on way to make something functional while immersing themselves in the creative process.

**Alice Hughes of the Alice Jane Studio** studied painting at the Glasgow School of Art. She describes how creating wearable, ornamental ceramics allows her to satisfy that tactile urge to *make* while bolstering her love of painting.

**Under the name Manifesto, Katie Rose Johnston** creates home ceramics. By designing innovative ways to integrate floral and multisensory elements such as incense into ceramics, she embodies her floral namesake. Katie believes in:

- a world of colour and play
- a culture of sustainable living and conscious consumption
- the sensory enjoyment of the hand-made.

Living and working in Scotland has undeniably been a big influence on my work. I think that some of my more recent pieces have taken on more organic forms and tones which stem from living in such a beautiful country. I'm also really encouraged by the writings of artists such as Paul Klee and Hans Arp who often create abstraction inspired by natural forms. I love using clay as it's such a raw material. It feels like such an ancient process to mould clay, fire it and make something that can be simultaneously functional and decorative.

ALICE HUGHES, ALICE JANE STUDIO

> Glass is easily ignored. We look through it, drink from it, admire our reflection in it, adjust our lenses and take it for granted.

JILL TURNBULL, SCOTTISH GLASS EXPERT

# THROUGH THE LOOKING GLASS

The first mention of glass in Britain is the glazing of the windows of a church at Monkwearmouth, Durham, which was completed in the year 674. The first glass-maker in Scotland was Sir George Hay, who was born in Perthshire. In 1610, he established the first blast furnace in Scotland from where he produced glass, soon gaining a monopoly over the trade.

The manufacture of glass containers can be traced back at least 400 years. However, it was only in the 19th century that commercial companies appeared on the scene. Among them was the Edinburgh and Leith Flint Glass Company, which was established in 1867. They changed their name in 1955 to the Edinburgh Crystal Company.

Unfortunately, the Edinburgh Crystal Company went bust in 2006, but they donated the equipment (lathes) used for their particular glass cutting technique to the Edinburgh College of Art. Glass cutting is now a heritage craft that embellishes the glass, creating cut-out patterns with different profile wheels encrusted with diamonds. It's a technique that creates precise patterns and freehand mark-making alike.

**Juli Bolaños-Durman is an artist and designer** who capitalised on ECA's unique glass-cutting equipment and has since created stunning sculptural pieces out of recycled glass. For her, glass is amazing to work with as it can 'be fixed' through the different processes; hand-cutting can transform a discarded glass into something precious. Juli's works share a visual similarity with the original output of the Edinburgh Crystal Company. Playful and poetic, they are acts of memory and imagination whose bright colours make them feel both historical and contemporary in design.

## TEXTURAL HEALING

You can't help but meditate on the industrial history of Scotland while walking past old factories, mills and industrial areas such as the Clydeside in Glasgow or Leith in Edinburgh. But for me, no reminder of Scottish industry is more prominent than the presence of Scottish woven fabrics – tartan, wool and tweed – in the home, whether these are the fabric of an upholstered sofa, a footstool, curtains or even a blanket wrapped around the body to ward off that moment when you need to turn on the central heating.

Some strands of contemporary Scottish knitwear follow the traditional design signposts of historic Scottish textiles, while others preserve the significance of historic fabrics as they expand to incorporate technological and international influences.

Coorie Bookshelf

*Landing Light*
Don Paterson

**Hilary Grant** is a design studio and partnership between Hilary Grant and Robert Harvey, founded in 2011. The partnership creates woollen products by using a family-run knitwear manufacturer in the Scottish Borders to produce their collections from Premium Geelong lambswool. The Geelong fibres are grown to a 'responsible wool standard' – before being spun and dyed on the east coast of Scotland. The tapestry-like visuals of the Hilary Grant range, which they describe as showcasing a 'relaxed orderliness', speak to the grid-like makeup of traditional tartan while also softly pointing towards the patterning of pixels and geometric forms that are reflected in contemporary architecture and design.

Up until the mid-19th century, textiles relied on the colours found in the landscapes in which they were created. Entirely natural dyes, made from heathers and grasses of the local area, would vary from season to season and place to place: there was little uniformity or consistency. Even when synthetic dyes were introduced, Scottish textiles continued to reflect the colours of the natural world.

**Catherine MacGruer** harnesses this aspect of Scottish design and incorporates it into her strikingly modern cushions, rugs and blankets. Through the minimalist patterns, block shapes, lines and forms portrayed, the use of forest greens, mustard yellows and russet oranges is a continuous theme.

## WARM FEET, WARM HEART

Hotties, or hot-water bottles, are a must for cold Scottish winters (and summers), especially in high-ceilinged, draughty tenements. Heat therapy is great for easing aches as well as for creating that snugly, coorie feeling of toasty comfort, so it isn't a surprise that hotties are a perennial favourite in many Scottish homes.

**Lucy Donnell** brings together the simple hot-water bottle and the luxurious warmth of British-spun lambswool to create vibrant pieces that are also downright handy.

Her hot-water bottles in their wee striped covers are part of Lucy's Para Handy collection, inspired by the busy harboursides and by the colour and light of the beautiful west coast of Scotland.

# Dressing Gown or Housecoat?

## What is the style of coorie?

 6

## PSYCHOLOGY OF COSY

It wouldn't be difficult to write a whole psychology textbook about our wardrobes, from the nostalgia captured in a single ragged T-shirt, to optimistic projections of our future selves in a sharply cut suit. The slight misconception of a phenomenon such as coorie is that you have to spend a lot of time and money changing what was there before. I would suggest that this is simply not true. At its heart, coorie is modest, comforting and familiar – it doesn't require the super-luxe, nor does it insist you spend money unnecessarily; rather you can work with and adapt what you have.

In assessing the coorie-ness or otherwise of your existing wardrobe, start by looking at what clothes you have, take note of what keeps you warm, is made of natural, breathable fabrics and, most importantly, what makes you feel good. Whether it's a striped cotton scarf you knitted yourself, or a chunky pair of woollen socks, a sturdy pair of beautifully worn-in walking boots or a vintage Fair Isle cardigan, think about your clothes afresh from a cosy coorie perspective and you might find hidden treasures to fall in love with again!

As if to give extra weight to these feelings, I discovered that a 2012 study published in the *Journal of Experimental Social Psychology* had coined the phrase 'embodied cognition' to describe how we think not just with our brains but also with our bodies.

## HOW TO EDIT . . . YOUR WARDROBE

As the plethora of decluttering lifestyle gurus indicates, we do have a 21st-century issue with hoarding. Apparently we only wear 20% of the clothing we own. A straightforward solution to this problem would be to downsize the actual physical size of our wardrobes and storage systems: the simple act of creating spatial constraints in the home can help us set limits on the amount of *stuff* we have. And, of course, a carefully edited selection of items is much easier to display and manage than heaps of ill-fitting, unloved and joyless clothes.

In a parallel version of Parkinson's Law where 'work expands to fill the time available for its completion', the dreaded stuff seems to magically expand to fill the space we make available to it. Somehow it seems easier to hold on to 'soft' goods (such as clothes) rather than 'hard' goods (such as appliances) – with the latter, unless you are a seriously committed hoarder, you're unlikely to have two coffee makers in your kitchen.

Perhaps this is because we convince ourselves that clothes don't take up as much space. However, by donating, swapping or recycling as much clothing as possible – and by buying vintage, second-hand or pre-loved – we can feed into the cycle of sustainable awareness, while also paring back on the volume of physical items we have in our homes.

## TARTANISATION

Are tartan comforts, housecoats and woollen jumpers distinctly Scottish? Unravelling the meanings behind Scottish sartorial choices is tricky. There's a complex history at play here, a multiplicity of influences – from the rest of the UK and beyond into Northern Europe – plus conflicting views on what Scottish national identity might consist of. Even so, I would suggest there is a definite Scottish 'look' when it comes to fashion that people from Tokyo to Toronto can recognise.

## WHERE'S YER HOUSECOAT?

What then does one wear when in pursuit of cosiness and comfort? Outflanked only by the ketchup vs brown sauce row, the housecoat vs dressing gown debate seems to be one of the most divisive regional arguments; it's lasted decades – at least in my house! – and is still going strong. Nonetheless we can all agree that, despite the difference in name, they are definitely comfy and essential.

What *is* a housecoat you ask? In most of western Scotland, it is simply an alternative name for a dressing gown. People from the rest of Scotland and the UK might see a housecoat as something similar to a work overcoat or overall, a comfortable, easy-to-wash garment that

Coorie Bookshelf

*The Secret Life of Tartan*
Vixy Rae

one might wear to protect your clothing while doing domestic work. Those of you of a certain age will perhaps remember your grandmother wearing one as she swept the back yard or cleaned the windows.

The contemporary Scottish housecoat is a garment you can readily buy from most high-street retailers, and at the same time the name and style is making its way into the forefront of Scottish design. For example, Glasgow-based designer Faisal Mohammed started an ethical clothing label for men called Cloh, through which he makes garments in which to lounge and chill that also offer the elegance of a high-end look. Faisal's sleek take on the housecoat succeeds in connecting cosiness and style.

> I want my garments to relieve stress and make the wearer feel peaceful and comfortable. Everything is handmade in Glasgow. Throughout the design process, every inch of available fabric is used to reduce wastage.

FAISAL MOHAMMED, CLOH

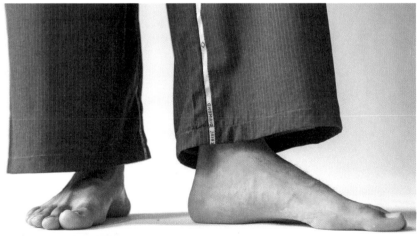

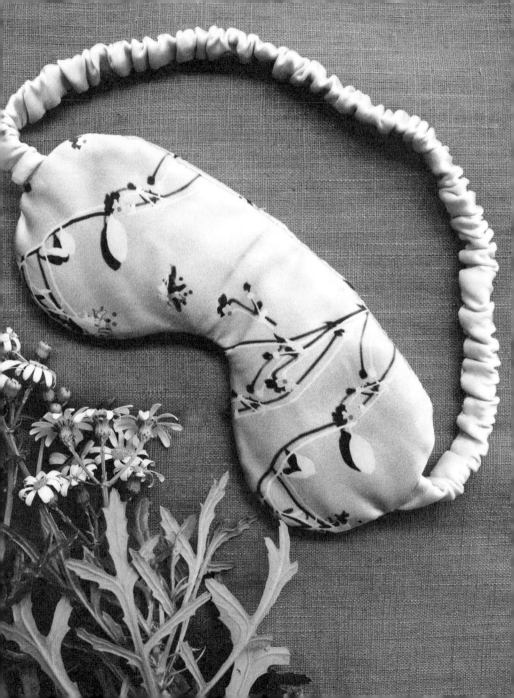

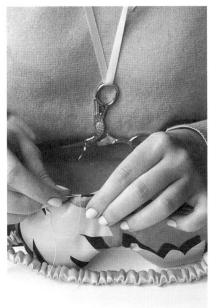

## SÒLAS

Another fantastic example of a fresh update of the housecoat is SÒLAS Sleepwear. SÒLAS, a small brand also based in Glasgow, specialises in luxury silk sleepwear. With a name that means light, comfort and joy in Gaelic, SÒLAS is a collaboration between duo Ruth Mitchell and Ciorstaidh Monk.

Ruth is a photographer and print designer who creates the printed fabric; Ciorstaidh is a designer and producer for Fashion Foundry, which designs the garment shapes. In the summer of 2017,

they decided to start making luxury sleepwear. Ciorstaidh began developing elegant loungewear shapes that would function as more public-facing clothing, too; the designs feature deep pockets and comfortable silhouettes. Ruth designed the prints based on her nostalgic memories of childhood and nature.

Both women spent a lot of time outdoors when they were growing up, Ciorstaidh on Benbecula and Ruth on the west coast near Glasgow, so they wanted to use these memories and emotional connections to make fabrics with a story behind them; their fabrics are personal and inherently Scottish, with a modern direction.

Since 2018, Ruth and Ciorstaidh have developed smaller, more affordable items, and they've made careful progress with the collection. SÒLAS prioritise not being wasteful; they use leftover fabric for sleep masks, scrunchies and covered buttons.

SÒLAS seek to work with people in Scotland as much as possible, including graphic designers, photographers, printers, garment makers and design collectives. They have collaborated with other creatives on projects such as a sleep spray with local fragrance studio Arboretum; a window display at Welcome Home with Paper Street Dolls; and events, such as that at the Hair Club, to launch their scrunchie in March 2019.

Ruth and Ciorstaidh believe these patterns of collaboration and experimentation are a great creative outlet, one which continues to inspire their work.

"Being in Glasgow is a really good place for us, it is a relatively small city and it's easy to get to know people. It's a very encouraging environment for new creative projects, and it's not difficult to find people to collaborate on ideas. Being close to the countryside and numerous parks and gardens provides us with the inspiration to make our designs but also the city provides a slightly faster pace and excitement. Scotland is endlessly inspiring with a rich textile history, and we're full of new ideas for the future."

RUTH MITCHELL, SÒLAS

## ALIVE AND WOOL

Let's take a moment to praise wool, which is enjoying a rightful revival. After decades of manmade unpleasantness, people are again prioritising wool in their work – and leisure – wardrobes. Here are some of its brilliant qualities.

1. Wool is beautifully wrinkle-resistant thanks to the fibre's springy structure which helps it keep its shape. For example, shirts made of wool can happily last for days of wear without needing any attention from an iron.

2. Wool has an excellent absorption rate which makes it naturally odour resistant.

3. Wool is a natural insulator that will keep you warm in the colder months, while its breathable qualities will keep you cool in the heat of summer. This makes it a clear favourite among athletes such as mountain climbers and hill runners who, just like early Arctic explorers, love a thin woollen base layer.

4. Wool is significantly more durable than many other fibres. Tests show that wool fibres resist tearing and can bend back on themselves more than 20,000 times without breaking. The figure for cotton is a mere 3,200 times.[i]

Multipurpose items such as blankets that double as scarves, or beautiful woollen socks that are great as slippers or as super-cosy boot liners are undeniably Scottish. They unite the outside and the inside. It's not surprising that many contemporary makers of wearable goods in Scotland choose to create pieces that are fitting for the most coorie of homes and further afield. Clothing so comfortable that you wouldn't hesitate to choose to wear it to coorie-in is golden.

The absolute winner is that these pieces are attainable for all budgets and tastes. Scots are renowned for their frugal approach to the central heating – and if you're broke then you certainly aren't turning it on until it actually snows.

This frugality makes a necessity of cosy loungewear and means that many of us have an ever-shifting collection of old woollen jumpers that are both functional and visually interesting.

The best knitted jumper or cardigan inhabits a space outside of gender norms. This might not always be the case in mainstream commercial settings, but the deep appeal of second-hand or vintage knitwear visions is that they can be worn beautifully by anyone, in a way that's similar to tartan clothing. Neither male nor female, the traditional knitwear of the Fair Isle is an intricate, evocative combination of colour and geometric pattern to create a story that's uniquely visual and tactile.

*The Diary of a Bookseller*
Shaun Bythell

# THE LASTING LEGACY OF WOOL

When investing in woollen products, it's good to choose something that will stand the test of time – in terms of its look and its durability. Scottish men often acquire a kilt at 21 that they will keep for life, and smaller items of clothing need be no different. My understanding is that, collectively, contemporary Scottish design is working against the global culture of throwaway clothing. Like generations before, there is now more of an emphasis on making things to last.

For centuries men wore hose socks with their kilts, held in place by garters adorned with flashes. The flashes are for show, but the socks harken back to those earlier times when elastic was not in the picture as a means of preventing the saggy-stocking look.

The *Sgian Dubh*, a small, single-edged knife, literally means 'black knife' but has an alternative meaning suggestive of covert or hidden (in the same way as the phrase 'black market' does). In the normal course of things, a weapon was often concealed under the armpit or within the folds of the kilt, but on entering a friend's house it was taken out and placed in the sock so as to be visibly non-threatening. And there it remains to this day.

There's no need for weapons, concealed or otherwise to enjoy a good pair of woollen socks. They're comfy, warm, stop your boots rubbing and – in extreme Baltic circumstances – will stop your feet getting frostbite. Whether you're going out or staying in, they elevate your everyday coorie life.

**Hose knitting** became established in Scotland in the 17th century and was strong in Haddington where the New Mills Company was set up in 1681. Stocking making also took place in many other parts of Scotland in the mid-1700s – including Glasgow, Edinburgh, Dumfries, Aberdeen and even in Stonehaven from where, as history relates, two stocking makers participated in the 1745 Jacobite uprising. By 1771 it was a well-established industry in the Scottish Borders, and one in which knitting machines and hand knitters worked side by side despite the invention of a knitting machine as long ago as 1589, which enabled socks to be knitted six times faster than by hand.

## THE JOY OF THE PERFECT SOCK

Rosie Sugden's fashion-forward designs reflect the 'made to last' ideology. Her accessories line combines her idiosyncratic take on contemporary design with the inherent natural beauty of Scottish cashmere, brought out through extraordinary craftsmanship. For example, Rosie's cashmere bed socks are knitted on a 60-year-old tubular machine, hand cut and then the toe seam is stitched together on a linking machine. They are an amazing treat for your feet during a bitingly cold and bleak Scottish winter!

Rosie is passionate about delivering the idea of coorie worldwide; her accessories are stocked all over Europe, and further afield in Japan. It is fantastic that the crafted products of a small Edinburgh-based company are available in outlets such as Liberty's, Fortnum & Mason and Bloomingdales. These irresistibly cosy woollen socks, shawls and scarves are a contemporary articulation of a Scottish heritage that refuses to stay in the past.

# BETH AND CIARA INTERVIEW
# ROSIE SUDGEN
## A ROUND-UP

**For you, how do inside and outside wear interchange?**

Outdoor wear can be really practical, adventure-style clothing or more often than not workwear which is usually worn to reflect a smart, professional appearance rather than comfort and cosiness. Either way, after a long day outside or in the office, I think everyone has that moment when they come home and want to 'get comfy', whether you're heading into the garden, doing some cooking, having a hot bath or simply flopping on to the sofa. It's about relaxing in your space, relishing the simple things and learning how to switch off: comfortable clothing can help you make that transition mentally and physically.

**What does coorie mean to you?**

To me it's a very comforting feeling, a mixture of warmth and contentment, in knowing that there is nowhere else you need to, or would rather, be. You're with people you love, or you're having quiet time alone to reflect and

recharge. Personally, after a long day in my studio, I love to be at home in Edinburgh on a cosy winter night curled up with a book, my two pugs, cashmere socks on, a cup of tea and some chocolate to hand.

**What does Scottishness look and feel like?**

I'm sure it can be many things to many people, but to me it's space to be yourself. Scotland is a very open and accepting place to live, in my experience, and I also think there is an element of adventure in Scottishness. It's one of the most beautiful places to live and there are so many adventures to be had and places to explore. I find that really intoxicating.

**Your bed socks demonstrate a lovely connection between the home and clothing. What other garments, which one might wear at home, show us what coorie is about?**

Definitely our ribbed shawl scarf. It's a really versatile piece that can be worn out and about

or indoors; during the colder months I wear mine around the clock. It's great for bundling up in outside and then, when you come inside and unravel the scarf, it transitions perfectly into a large shawl. I designed it to be quite wide so that when worn as a scarf it's thick and insulating, and when worn as a shawl you have that lovely feeling of it being wrapped around your shoulders.

**Why is making garments in Scotland significant to you?**
I think 'Made in Scotland' is a stamp of quality known across the world. I've grown up around the Scottish textile industry and there is such a wealth of skills here as well as a rich manu-facturing history. My yarn is from Scottish spinners and is knitted up at a family-run mill in the Borders – it wouldn't occur to me to manufacture anywhere else.

**How do makers such as yourself acknowledge historical Scottish design in very contemporary pieces?**
All my designs are made in Scotland and I am lucky enough to work with people whose families have been part of the industry for generations. So, a lot of these skills have been passed down. We combine that with the new technology of Shima Seiki machines and the cashmere's inherent natural beauty, and I think that's what makes the product so special. Equally we have two designs, our best-selling turbans and ear-warmers, which are still hand-frame knitted as this is the only way to achieve the chunky stitch and snug fit. They are designed for modern life but made using a technique which is hundreds of years old.

## A CUP OF TEA, A SOFT BLANKET AND A BIT OF QUIET

The Tartan Blanket Co. believes slow living is not just a collection of nice moments but rather an act of great daring. For co-founders Emma and Fergus Macdonald, choosing peace over pressure in the face of endless to-do lists, unhung laundry and life's inevitable chaos is a learned art and was a large part of the decision to leave their jobs in London in 2014. With dreams of creating a business that balanced doing what they loved with the family life they had always dreamed of, they returned home to Edinburgh.

### COLSIE / kol-zee
origin: Old Scots for 'cosy'

1. The habit of embracing winter darkness and finding comfort and warmth in life's simple pleasures.
2. The feeling that comes with being present, inviting closeness and appreciating the things that last.
3. The act of slow living and making time for the people and things that soothe our souls.

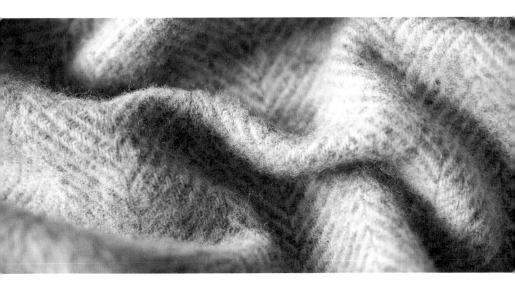

What followed was a lot of hard work and learning how to best use each other's skills. With Fergus's background in business and the highland-wear industry, and Emma's experience in fashion buying and merchandising, they saw a unique opportunity to introduce a design-led approach to traditional Scottish goods and so the Tartan Blanket Co. was born. In a renovated warehouse in Leith, a creative hub nestled among old docks, the company is surrounded by its primary source of inspiration: the deep chill and long nights of Scottish winters.

From the rolling hills of the rainy Highlands to the cobbled streets of Edinburgh, their collection seeks to merge the colours and textures of Scotland into a contemporary line that welcomes style and warmth into the home. Breaking away from the more traditional tartans, they are known for their limited-edition designs that revisit classic weaving techniques with modern colourways and patterns in a variation of wool types.

With firm favourites such as their Recycled Wool Blankets (70% wool and 30% recycled fibres saved from landfill), this is a blanket company that places an emphasis on the sustainable, breathable and timeless benefits of wool.

## SHOES AFF

Footwear and lack thereof can speak volumes – there is a reason many people associate relaxation and pleasure with walking barefoot along a beach. While bare feet aren't always ideal, especially in a gritty urban setting, a recent study demonstrates that the skin on the soles of your feet can resist abrasions and blistering.[ii] As the trend for 'barefoot running' indicates, not to mention the flexible feet of yoga devotees, going barefoot can benefit the musculoskeletal structure of your feet and ankles. It's argued that kicking off your shoes can help prevent foot injuries. We all know those who like to sit at their desks free from the cast-like structure of their shoes, many of which hold the bones of the foot so rigid that they can't move fluidly. This can cause the foot to become passive and lose the ability to support itself. Going barefoot can enable your feet to readapt themselves, to become stronger and more flexible, realigning your entire posture.

As with the layering of throws and blankets in an interior that undulates with the Scottish seasons, footwear, too, can be built up or reduced like layers for your feet. Try bare feet for those precious warmer days, and house shoes, socks or slippers when the temperature drops. (A word of warning – going barefoot will soon alert you to the cleanliness or other-wise of your coorie home's flooring!)

## BAFFIES – WHAT ARE THEY?

Baffies, the Scottish word for slippers, is thought to derive from the Scots word *bachle*, meaning old shoe or worn-out shoe – and are therefore only worn in the house. They have gained linguistic ground during the last century and the 'Transactions of the Scottish Dialects Committee' (1914), refers to baffies many times, defining them as 'old loose slip-pers', perhaps the opposite of those more rigid shoes we often wear to work.

# Felt your own baffies

This might sound tricky but all you're doing is using a foot-shaped template and covering it in wool and water a few times over until you create a slipper. Imagine papier mâché with wool and you'll soon get the hang of it!

## You will need:

a pair of beach shoes or plastic shoes
 (a couple of sizes larger than your own
 shoe size – they will not be damaged in the
 process)
35g natural wool roving
 (this is wool that has yet to be spun into yarn;
 perfect for felting, it can be found at a craft
 supply shop)
a bar of plain soap
hot water
a cheesegrater
a pair of tights (ordinary 'nylons')
a spray bottle

## Method:

1. Fill a spray bottle with hot water. Grate some soap into it. Wait until the soap has dissolved, creating lightly soapy water.
2. Spray some soapy water onto the sole of your first shoe.
3. Take a length – about the length of the shoe – of the wool roving.
4. Lay it flat over the base of the shoe, so the sole is covered. Dampen the wool with the hot water and press it down and into the shoe with your hands. Smooth out any uneven areas using water and the same downwards-pressing motion.
5. Working from the sole up, cover the shoe in water and wool roving.
6. Repeat this process two to three more times, depending on how thick you want your slipper.
7. For Round 2, smooth the wool in the opposite direction to Round 1; likewise with Round 3.
8. Repeat the process on the second shoe.
9. Once the shoes are covered in at least two layers of thick wool roving, they should feel quite firm. If not, smooth the wool down until it sticks strongly together.
10. Next, cut the feet off your tights to create long 'socks'. Insert each wool-covered shoe into a 'sock' and knot the ends securely.
11. Place the socks with the slippers-to-be into the tumble dryer for five to ten minutes.
12. Then unknot the socks and gently remove your shoes from inside the baffies.
13. If the baffies have shrunk too much, plunge into hot water to loosen the wool and try again.
14. Now your baffies are ready to be worn!

# You'll Have Had Your Tea

# 7

## Hospitality in the home

I have always found Scottish people, whether friends, family or near-strangers, to be among the most welcoming I have ever encountered, constantly going above and beyond to make their guests feel comfortable and at home. When I have stayed with Scots, even if I haven't known them before meeting them, the idiom 'offering the shirt off one's back' feels very apt. And it seems that Scottish hospitality forms part of an ancient tradition. There is evidence that Scotland welcomed in and traded with central Europeans as far back as the Iron Age, before even the Romans came to Scotland.

## AW KINDS OF FOLK

The Scots, like many other nations, are proud to take hospitality very seriously.

> "Where they shall not onely feede but feast, and not feast but banket. This is a man whose greatest cares are to practise the workes of piety, charity, and hospitality."

**PETER HUME BROWN**
*EARLY TRAVELLERS IN SCOTLAND*

Some Scottish homes have evolved from the open-plan spaces such as those commonly found in the Highlands and Islands to be formed of separate, perhaps smaller rooms. In the historically open crofts, food was cooked and served from the same area where everyone slept, with the human inhabitants almost certainly breathing the same air as the livestock from which some of the ingredients came. Granted some Scottish-designed dwellings are now upholding this same freedom of space as well as a self-sustainable outlook – though minus the living-room livestock!

In more closed-plan homes, despite their names remaining the same, the contents of the dining room and kitchen have changed throughout time. A remarkable phenomenon of the Scottish middle-class home between about 1760 and 1810 was the value placed upon the dining table with its matching set of chairs. This ensemble of furniture came to dominate the living space in terms of both its physical size and its expense. In tenement flats with no more than four or five rooms, visitors would often be greeted by a multi-leaved table surrounded by 12 or 16 chairs.

From the wood that these furniture sets were made of to the foods served in the 18th and 19th centuries, nearly everything spoke of the trading boom in Scotland. Of course, this 'boom' depended upon the international reach of the British Empire; benefits for the people of Scotland were gained at the expense of others' exploitation and oppression. The mahogany in their tables and the rum in their glasses of punch were two of the most valuable commodities in Scotland's Atlantic trades – of which slavery was a significant part – and at the core of the vast business wealth that changed the face of Glasgow. Scottish hospitality has been shaped by forces positive and negative; it's vital to acknowledge these if we are to partake in it with honesty and integrity.

Coorie Bookshelf

*Scots Cooking: The Best Traditional and Contemporary Scottish Recipes*
Sue Lawrence

# A PLACE TO GATHER

Hosting friends and family is a huge part of Scottish culture. From the Highlands to the Lowlands, whether it is a cuppa or a ceilidh, our homes are always up for the challenges and rewards of playing the convivial role of host. Every inch of space, every table, chair and rug are often shifted around, stacked, expanded or rolled away to accommodate a larger number of people.

It would be fair to say that in the majority of Scottish homes – as with many others around the world – every object present serves a purpose, and often two or three purposes. All available space is put to work; a spare room might double up as a home office, for example. The settee that miraculously transforms into a bed when you want it to be; the side table that heralds your clattering keys as you get home can, on a special occasion, serve as your mini bar.

Yes, decorative elements such as photographs and paintings are present as aesthetic additions, but these too help celebrate community and the beauty that surrounds us in the landscape or act as memorandums from times past. This multiplicity of meaning and use perhaps stems from the many times when Scotland's population simply couldn't afford more than what was necessary.

It feels to me like a unique take on minimalism that has shaped how contemporary homes look and perform today, even when many of the most functional homes don't visually translate as minimal in their aesthetic. This by no means distinguishes what is great about Scottish hospitality, but it does mean that it's uniquely presented.

## DINNER TIME

> At his house was
> true hospitality;
> a simple but a
> plentiful table;
> and every guest,
> being left at
> perfect freedom,
> felt himself quite
> easy and happy.
>
> **JAMES BOSWELL**
> *THE JOURNAL OF A TOUR*
> *TO THE HEBRIDES*

Sharing a meal makes brilliant practical sense and is good for the soul, too. Eating in the company of others can be a true act of community and, in environmental terms, reduces food waste. Regular, shared mealtimes bring rhythm and pattern to our lives. The sense they offer of togetherness and familiarity can evoke deep feelings of contentment and security, the sustaining memories of which may form the basis of future rituals with new or blended sets of family and friends.

In all environments and stages of life, human beings need structure and routine. At their best, mealtimes have a meditative, joyful quality. They offer people the opportunity to stop, to sit still psychologically and literally, to reflect on their day and days ahead, and to listen to and interact with others. Mealtimes can be a grounding opportunity – a time when anxieties can be expressed and you can be listened to. Shared laughter and sustenance often follow.

## BAKING BEAUTIES

People having pals over for a cup of tea became common practice in Scotland in the early 1800s and now feels like the most inclusive hospitality practised. Young or old, rich or poor, we are united with a brew. 'Scottish breakfast tea' or Scottish blends are subtle personal touches that separate this from the English cuppa. Again, it means so much more when you stop in for tea with someone else. The idea of voicing one's fears and being vulnerable may seem daunting, but the ritual of drinking tea (or coffee!) with others creates a space to do so comfortably. It's a tradition that's worth nurturing.

My gran used the same biscuit tin for decades, and it was always a lottery moment when it was opened. We never knew if she'd been busy with her home baking and, if she had, we felt like we'd hit the jackpot.

Baking sometimes seems like a cornerstone of the UK's national identity, as you'll know if you have binge-watched *The Great British Bake Off*. It's loved by all ages and people from all walks of life. I spoke to Ronan Sinclair (@chasingthe-doughnut_), who bakes beautiful, irresistible cakes for small cafés in Edinburgh. She says:

> I love putting cakes in front of people and seeing their faces light up! I like to be the hostess and I'm a bit of a feeder so baking really is a good fit for me.

# SHORTBREAD

Scottish favourites include pancakes, scones, fruit cakes, oatcakes and shortbread. The story of Scottish shortbread begins with the medieval 'biscuit bread'. Leftover dough from bread making was dried out in a low oven until it hardened into a rusk: the word 'biscuit' means 'twice cooked'. As butter came to replace the yeast in the bread, this 'biscuit bread' developed into shortbread. At that time shortbread was too expensive for ordinary people; it was reserved as a special treat for occasions such as weddings, Christmas and New Year.

Shortbread's significance is highlighted by historic traditions that have grown up around it. In Shetland there's a tradition of breaking a decorated shortbread cake over the head of a new bride on the threshold of her new home. The custom of eating shortbread at New Year has its origins in the ancient pagan 'yule cakes', which symbolised the sun. And it is still traditionally offered to 'first footers' on New Year's Day.

Shortbread is also ubiquitous; it can be as cheap as chips, as plain or as sumptuous as you like. But to make it is neither costly nor difficult. If you are in a worry about what to bake for a pal's visit or a charity bake sale, shortbread is your go-to as it can be made with only three ingredients – butter, sugar, flour – although every culinary celebrity tends to put their own fancy twist on it.

# Shortbread recipe

**For a bake that you'd be proud to take to the in-laws, try the following recipe.**

**You can easily make vegan shortbread by using vegan butter or margarine in place of the dairy butter.**

**You will need:**
50g caster sugar, plus extra for sprinkling
100 butter, cubed
150g plain flour, plus extra for dusting

**Method:**
1. Preheat your oven to 170°C.
2. In a large mixing bowl, combine the ingredients and use your hands to work the mixture into a dough.
3. Using a rolling pin, roll out the dough on a floured work surface until it has a thickness of around 1cm.
4. Cut the dough into a shape of your choice. For a traditional shortbread, cut the dough into fingers and use a fork to prick the surface of each biscuit.
5. Place the biscuits on a lined baking tray and chill in the fridge for around 20 minutes, until the dough feels firm.
6. Bake in the oven for 15–20 minutes until they begin to turn golden brown.
7. Remove from oven, sprinkle on caster sugar and leave to cool.

## YOU'LL HAVE HAD YOUR TEA

While the warmth and conviviality of
Scottish hospitality have – hopefully – not
diminished over the centuries, our eating
habits have certainly altered. Instead of
resorting to processed meals filled with
preservatives and additives, we now
have the opportunity to return to the
ingredients raised and grown on Scottish
soil and treat them with the respect they
were accorded in times of poverty and
lack. In combination with the diversity
of ingredients we can now enjoy, this
offers a chance to revitalise and refresh
Scottish fare.

    Traditional Scottish cooking prides
itself on being simple, healthy, unintimi-
dating and unpretentious; accessible to
everyone, rich and poor. Everyone can
understand the sentiment, if not quite
all the words, in this verse from Burns's
famous poem about egalitarianism, 'A
Man's a Man for A' That', written after
the French Revolution (with which Burns
sympathised), in 1795.

> What though on hamely fare we dine,
> Wear hoddin grey, an' a that,
> Gie fools their skills, and knaves their wine;
> A Man's a Man for a' that.

## GRAINS OF TRUTH

As our past suggests, food in Scotland is at once simple and intricate, sourced both near and far. Owing to the far reach of historical trading, the legacy of colonialism and the dynamic mix of cultures that exist in Scotland today, we don't have to eat nothing but porridge anymore (thank goodness!). But we do have to acknowledge that grains have played a huge part in nourishing the Scottish people. Meat hasn't always been accessible to everyone, but grains have been a consistent food group for rich, poor and everyone in between thanks to their long shelf life and affordability.

**Bere (pronounced bear)** is a well-loved grain in the Highlands and Islands. An ancient grain, it was eaten by the Neolithic inhabitants of Skara Brae over 5,000 years ago. Its current popularity is perhaps thanks to the old wife's tale that has come to light that bere bread or 'miracle bread' helps ease the symptoms of the menopause.

**Spelt flour** also makes for a cracking loaf of bread, and spelt grain has been found in the archaeological remains of a crannog in Loch Tay, an Iron Age site dating to approximately 500 BCE. A form of wheat that was thought to have been brought over in the Roman invasion of

Britain in the 1st century AD, the presence of spelt in Scotland – 500 years earlier than expected – suggests that the Iron Age Scots were an advanced society with wealth and trading routes across Europe.

**Over the centuries, Scottish oats** as a staple of the national diet have come in for a lot of flak. But the strength of their longevity is indicated by the timeless heritage packaging that certain brands of 'porage' oats still use and, more obscurely by the 14th-century French chronicler Jean Froissart's observation of Scots soldiers carrying bags of oatmeal to make their own oatcakes.

Today the humble oats have undergone a makeover, as evidenced by the proliferation of flapjacks, bircher muesli (porridge soaked overnight with grated apple), pots of instant porridge and hipster cafés offering Insta-worthy bowls of porridge adorned with 'fresh seasonal fruit and honey'. The current fashionability of oats is partly because of the reach of the GI diet, which promotes foods with a low glycaemic index. As ultra-distance runners, impoverished students and the parents of small children have long known, porridge is an excellent, thrifty source of complex carbohydrates, which release energy slowly into the bloodstream.

I love the versatility of porridge: it caters happily to all dietary requirements. Oats are wholegrain, can be made with any milk or milk alternative of your choice and are entirely free of the sugars and other additives present in processed cereals. They can lower cholesterol, reduce constipation and minimise the risk of diabetes. There are lots of other benefits claimed, too – I'm happy to vouch for the hangover-easing one, for sure.

Oats are also thought to ease depression; I'm sure the unhurried, calming ritual of measuring out and stirring a bowl of porridge offers a daily boost to wellbeing. There is even a special tool designed for this task – the 'spurtle' is a lovely, smooth wooden stick dating back to the 15th century. If you're serious about your porridge, your coorie kitchen will thank you for investing in one.

For me, oats in the form of porridge have always felt like an edible and delicious conjuring of the coorie ethos. The simplicity of the recipe – and the ways in which it can be adapted and enhanced to suit individual tastes (salt, anyone?) – means there isn't really a limit on how many can share the dish. Whether you are feeding one or one hundred, adjusting the oats to liquid ratio is easy. It's hard to get a pan of porridge wrong. And the warmth and sustenance that a bowl can bring is a multisensory manifestation of a hug; it's physical and emotional fuel for whatever the day will bring.

# Carrot Cake Porridge

My favourite food hacks happen when you can re-contextualise your favourite taste. Enter carrot cake porridge. Carrots have been around in Scotland for ever – and Scots have used them as natural sweeteners since the Middle Ages.

Carrot cake is an idea that was revived during rationing in World War Two, which now enjoys a fabulous, versatile reputation. (We have an even fresher spin on that old favourite – parsnip cake; not that I'll be trying parsnips on my porridge anytime soon.)

An added bonus is that carrots are super easy to grow if you're feeling green fingered. If not, they are some of the cheapest – and most readily available – finds on the fruit and veg aisle.

You will need:

For the porridge:
one or two carrots, depending on how big your carrots and portion sizes are
oats, ½ cup per person
milk or a milk substitute (for a total-bargain dish, water or a water/milk mix is perfect), ½ cup per person
spices of your choice (for a truly carrot cake flavour I use a combination of cinnamon, cardamom, cloves, nutmeg, allspice and ginger)

For the toppings (all delicious as a standalone or combined): honey, agave nectar, banana, chopped nuts, dried fruit and berries

Method:
1. Grate the carrots into a bowl.
2. Add your oats and milk.
3. Stir in your choice of spices.
4. Put the mixture into a saucepan (or the microwave if you must). Bring it to the boil and then simmer for 5 to 10 minutes, depending on how you like your oats.
5. Stir the mixture occasionally to prevent it from burning.
6. Spoon the porridge into a bowl and add your selection of toppings.
7. Sit down at your coorie dining table and enjoy!

> " There was a comfortable parlour with a good fire,
> and a dram went round. "

JAMES BOSWELL
*THE JOURNAL OF A TOUR TO THE HEBRIDES*

# A WEE TIPPLE

## WHISKY

It is an undisputed fact that Scots love a wee dram. Whether it actually warms you up is an ongoing debate . . . which I'm always happy to discuss. A nip of whisky never goes amiss and enjoying a drink together in the home is a well-practised way of coorie-ing in.

The word 'whisky' is perhaps the Latinised form of the Gaelic, commonly spelled *usquebaugh*, from *uisge beatha*, 'water of life'. From the 15th century, whisky was produced in small pot stills on farms or grain mills in the glens of the western Highlands and Islands of Scotland. The raw materials used were locally grown barley or bere, water which had flowed through peat, and peat itself for malting and as a fuel to heat the distilling apparatus.

The significance of whisky to Scottish culture and identity is something that can be both overstated and underrated. However, it is an indisputable fact that

its economic importance as a world brand – Scotch and single malt – is huge by any standard. There are many in Scotland whose livelihoods depend on the commercial success of the drink. In Scotland's north-east, home to many distilleries, the ritual of 'takin' a dram' has deep resonance at social gatherings.

Among whisky drinkers, the buying of drams for others is part of the inherent reciprocity of such occasions. It is not uncommon to see drinkers (most usually male) with a line of glasses in front of them containing 'nips' of whisky interspersed with the occasional half-pint of beer. When country people go visiting, the host may bring out a bottle to offer as part of the social ritual. Undoubtedly the drinking of whisky is equated with an assertion of regional and national identity. A dram or two is often accompanied by the singing of local songs such as bothy ballads. This happens at all tiers of formality: from weddings to a wee laugh around the table after a home-cooked dinner.

## BEER

Given that Scotland is such a multi-faceted country, locally produced drinks are almost certain to be more varied than whisky alone. Whether or not we are to believe that the Picts brewed beer from heather, there is no doubt that beer has been a common drink in Scotland for centuries. It seems to have been long enjoyed as a good and palatable beverage, as the author of an ancient Gaelic poem says:

I should like the angels of heaven to be drinking it through time eternal.

## GIN

More recently, Scotland has revamped its thirst for the juniper berry-based spirit, gin. Gin first arrived in Scotland from the Netherlands on the shores of Leith in the form of Dutch Genever; by 1777 there were a few legitimate distillers alongside 400 unregistered stills. The neutral spirit needed to produce gin is essentially made in the same way as whisky but distilled to a higher ABV (alcohol by volume). The mostly flavourless spirit is then infused or redistilled with any number of botanicals to make gin.

For many new distilleries, gin has proved a necessary, popular side hustle while they patiently wait for their whisky to mature. With its freshness and variety of flavours, gin enhances a wee night in, or a big do. It also resonates with Scottish history – from where it is made, following the tradition of repurposing old industrial buildings, to what it is made from.

Eden Mill Gin, for example, is made on the site of an old distillery on the banks of the River Eden, and their 'golf gin' is infused with shavings of hickory from 'retired golf clubs' as well as botanicals taken from the coastal courses of Scotland.

# THE ART OF FORAGING

When I asked an archaeologist what dietary lessons we can learn from our ancient ancestors, he said, without hesitation, 'live seasonally' – that is, eat local produce that is in season, and be aware of what your immediate environment has to offer at any given time of the year. Not all of us have a functional vegetable patch, access to an allotment or our own gardens, so a fantastic way to explore the seasonal life is to get into foraging.

Foraged berries, herbs, mushrooms and edible plants are extremely versatile, and can enhance what you eat and drink at home. It goes without saying that you need to make extra sure you know exactly what is safe to eat and what isn't.

Other than that, you don't need anything special to forage, just time and energy, plus some awareness of what is in season in Scotland (and what could poison you). Wild garlic will be the first thing available in the year, instantly recognisable by its distinctive smell. There's also nettles, mushrooms and brambles all readily available, with brambles often found in secret corners of the city – if you know where to look. But be quick; the best spots are soon depleted by jam and crumble aficionados. Elderflowers adorn the landscape for most of the summer, before turning into elderberries at the end of summer, start of autumn.

# Elderflower cordial

**This recipe will make about 4 litres of cordial.**

**You will need:**
20 elderflower heads, stalks removed
2 unwaxed lemons
500ml honey (local if possible)
2kg sugar
1.5l water
85g citric acid (a trip to your local wholefood
  store might be needed)

**Method:**
1. Put the water, sugar and honey in a large pan and cook over a low heat.
2. Once the sugar has dissolved, take the pan off the heat.
3. Add the elderflower to the mixture, ensuring the flowers are completely under the sugar water.
4. Grate the lemons, keeping the zest, and cut into slices.
5. Add the lemon slices, zest and citric acid to the mixture.
6. Cover and set the pan aside for 24 hours, leaving the cordial to infuse.
7. After 24 hours, line a sieve or colander with a clean tea towel or a piece of muslin.
8. Strain the mixture through the sieve/colander into another large pan or bowl.
9. Use a ladle to scoop the finished cordial into sterilised bottles or jars.
10. The cordial is ready to drink and can be stored in the fridge for up to six weeks. Enjoy!

A really generous tree – providing the fruit 'Sambucus Nigra' or Elderberry – it has been revered for millennia for its health giving and tasty offerings.

RUPERT WAITES, *BUCK & BIRCH*

# Spiced Bramble Gin

This is a great Christmas treat for two reasons. One, for the fab flavours and two, because it's a cracking gift, especially for the grannies! We've gone bramble picking since I was a child, and like any form of berry picking more go in the belly than the basket. Every autumn I still go. Even though I now live in the city, there are always bushes to be found lurking in unexpected places. Also, there is always someone who knows where a good haul is to be found. Each autumn I freeze some berries so that they last me into winter. I usually make my bramble gin in November with my frozen berries, so the mix will be ready by Christmas.

When I'm giving the gin out as presents, I like to make wee tags to accompany them and put some blackberries in with the gin to give it a pretty wee nod to its origins – but go wild and decorate as you wish!

You will need:
1 litre of gin
300g of foraged brambles (blackberries). You could change it up and use cranberries, though you need to prick them before using
250g sugar
cinnamon sticks
clementine peel
cloves
ginger
vanilla
bay leaves

Method:
1. Chuck all the ingredients in a sterilised, airtight container and shake until the sugar is dissolved.
2. Keep the container somewhere you can see it so you'll remember to turn it over/shake it a few times daily.
3. After a month of this . . . *voilà!* Strain the mixture through a sieve or colander and transfer the liquid into sterilised bottles.
4. Seal the bottles and drink . . . I mean give away to your nearest and dearest!

To serve:
1. Fill a tumbler with crushed ice and some brambles.
2. Pour over a serving of bramble gin and top up the glass with Prosecco.
3. Add a ring of clementine and a cinnamon stick for a final flourish.

Coorie Bookshelf

*Morvern Callar*
Alan Warner

# WASTE NOT WANT NOT

Once your guests have left, or gone to bed, after a dinner party or coorie gathering, you'll hopefully recycle your empties. But, if you are feeling creative, why not do what many Scots do and keep your bottles to reuse? Many hold on to their empties as a cross between decoration and trophy. Perhaps the latter isn't the healthiest attitude, so let's focus on the former.

After accumulating a selection of glass and ceramic vessels, plan a crafternoon to revamp your empties into functioning lamps, soap dispensers, vases or even turn a can into an aluminium stove for your next camping trip or barbecue. If you're lucky enough to have accrued bottle corks, these are brilliantly easy to turn into heatproof mats, garden markers, key chains and place holders for your next gathering.

# A Gid Bit of Fresh Air

Gardens, allotments and
connecting to nature

8

## THE LIGHT FANTASTIC

Any type of interaction with nature can be fruitful – from growing plants in pots on a windowsill to walking across miles of wild landscapes. Having access to some green space is nourishing in many ways – for example, spending time outside is proven to improve both your mental and physical health, increasing your quality of life and sense of wellbeing. And purposeful activity in the fresh air – whether it be hiking up a Munro, tending to the wisteria around your front door or gathering the wild garlic that grows along the towpath – can be so meditative and restorative as to help see you through the toughest of times.

Since the growing season in Scotland is compressed into fewer warmer months, Scots tend to make the most of this precious sun-kissed time by creating gardens known for their glorious appearances when in bloom. But why stop at gardens? From public parks, to old and new woodlands, allotments, glens and fields – Scotland is full of nourishing green spaces to explore and enjoy.

By the abundance of Scots words that reflect different kinds of light, you can bet that people in Scotland were historically fine-tuned to the nuanced shifts in seasons and patterning of daylight that indicate lives primarily lived outside amid the elements. Overleaf are a few favourites.

## MORNING-BLINK

noun

early morning light

## MORNING-MUN

noun

increasing daylight

## MIRK MONANDAY

noun

a day of uncommon darkness

## BEIK

verb

to bask in the sun

## DWAMING

verb

the fading of light

## NEUK-TIME

noun

the twilight; in reference to it being the season for down-time or gossiping among work people

## DIM

noun

midsummer twilight between sunrise and sunset

## BEAUTY THEN AND NOW

The Scots have been described as a 'nation of gardeners' since the 1750s when artistic horticultural pursuits became more common in Scotland. A fear of losing the beautiful attributes of historic Scottish gardens emerged during the Industrial Revolution when wealthy Scots decided to radically reinvent the gardens of large estates. Up came the old box hedging, down went the fruit espaliers, away goes the sundial. When every trace had been obliterated of what someone had planted with such enjoyment in went some monkey puzzle trees and the transformation was complete.

But luckily many gardens were saved. Contemporary Scotland has some of the best examples of the formal garden. Here there are true gardens of the past, reminiscent of Walter Scott's descriptions of aristocratic gardens, with great stone-walled enclosures, avenues of venerable trees, sculpted portals, courtyards, stone steps, sundials and towers.

Gardens, allotments and connecting to nature    **183**

# GARDENS FOR EVERYONE

Scotland's Garden Scheme facilitates open days across Scotland so everyone – gardeners or otherwise – can enjoy time in green spaces, whether it's an unusual garden on both sides of an old railway station platform, a bijou urban garden bursting with surprises or a traditional walled garden with Victorian green-houses, statuary and gazebos. The sheer variety and geographical reach of these gardens make for sunny, inspirational (and cheap) afternoons out – especially in the full bloom of June.

**Little Sparta** is a spectacular example. Located just south of Edinburgh, it was created by visual artist and gardener Ian Hamilton Finlay, and celebrates the joys of creativity and nature upon several acres of wild and exposed moorland.

## THE GREEN HOUSE

For those blessed with historical homes, it can be a challenge to sympathetically bring their accompanying gardens into the 21st century while at the same time upholding horticultural integrity and retaining their fantastic character. Real artistry and dedication are required.

A fine example of a reinvigorated historic garden is the Green House at Eskhill. Robin and Lindsay Burley, business coaches and founders of Eskhill & Co, had lived in Eskhill House for 22 years before building a new home in their kitchen garden. Using the site of a pre-existing greenhouse, they built the ecologically friendly and low-energy Green House. Their land features a 19th-century walled kitchen garden, paths still in the 1831 layout, maintaining the visual pattern of the original system of paths, and a sundial. The orchard, fruit garden, vegetable garden and a courtyard with shrub beds have been retained and symbolise the historical character of the property.

The Burleys find joy in maintaining the beautiful plants that have been growing in the garden for more than a hundred years, but they have also made their own additions. Lindsay cultivates tulips, flowers that she loves as the work they require is more than reciprocated when you can present them in a wee bouquet for friends and family rather than spend-ing on imported cut flowers.

Gardens, allotments and connecting to nature 185

## ROYAL FLOWERS

Mary Stuart (1542–1587) is known to have been very keen on flowers. She is said to have brought a wild rose, now named 'Mary Queen of Scots' in her honour, to Scotland from France in 1561. It's a charming rose with small, double flowers of purple and lilac-grey, paler on the outside. It's also extremely tough and can grow even in poor conditions.

Growing flowering plants can be a challenge in Scotland with rain, low temperatures, sporadic sunshine and high winds to contend with. But it can be done. Not only does cultivating a rich variety of plants in your garden – or any outside space you can nominate as your 'garden' – support local bees, but it's a great, sustainable source of decorative material for your home that will keep on giving. You do not need a large garden! I have seen the residents of tower blocks take over once scrubby patches of grass in front of their homes and create urban flowerbeds full of colour, care and ornament for everyone to enjoy.

Many annual flowers can be grown in a small space as long as it gets plenty of what daylight there is. And nearly all flowers thrive in fertile, well-nourished soil so the pleasingly earthy autumnal task of mulching with compost (homemade if possible) helps give them longevity.

# Ciara's tips for wreath making

I love a wreath. Lots of people pop them up at Christmas – and increasingly at Easter, too – but I think, why limit these beauties to the festive season? You can easily adapt them according to what's available at a particular time of year or do one of my favourite things, which is to create a selection of foliage and flowers and leave them to dry. The Scots have something of a reputation for being cautious with money and I am no exception . . . I see it less as being 'tight' and more as being 'efficient with resources'.

Crafting your own wreath from home-sourced foliage is cheap, cheerful and incredibly satisfying. My top tip for any craft project is to 'gie it laldy'. In other words: give it your all. Have fun, be imaginative and allow yourself to become absorbed in the flow of the task.

It's not about making it look perfect and glossy-magazine worthy. It's about experimenting, being yourself and feeling proud of what you've created. I like to remember how my mum's smile made me feel when I brought a pasta necklace home from nursery!

**You will need:**
a crafting ring – anything from a hula hoop to an embroidery hoop (you can get these for under £5 online)
foliage and flowers
garden wire/any malleable wire
secateurs
ribbon or twine
fresh moss (if doing a base layer)

**A note on foliage and flowers:**
I like to mix up what I am using. For foliage, I favour eucalyptus – the smell and silvery colour are absolutely my jam! But most fresh evergreens will work – something with a stalk that's a tad woodier.

You could also use fresh lavender, sage, bay, rosemary or curry leaves to add fun textures and smells. Florists can provide you with foliage, but I prefer to get out and about. Go out for a walk in your garden or along a hedgerow trail with a pair of scissors or secateurs and gather what you can find and go from there. But please make sure not to snip floral displays from the park or deplete wild flowers. You can always go to the florist to 'top up' what you have or to help make a variety. There are no hard and fast rules!

**Method:**

1. Start with your base. It's okay to use whatever you have to hand. It can be an official wire or wicker wreath base or something you already have. I've used an embroidery hoop before and hula hoops are ideal if you plan to make a larger wreath. The wider the hoop, the wider the wreath, but you can also build it up.

2. Attach the wire to the hoop and then tightly pack moss into small sections, securing with the wire. Continue round till the whole frame is covered. The moss can be optional if you want to keep it strictly floral. Or you can attach moss to the base to make it a bit fuller. This can be a good strategy if you've got less foliage or more flowers as it pads everything out and gives the wreath depth.

3. Take your florals and foliage and cut into roughly 20cm stalks. Obviously the sizing will vary according to the size of hoop you have. Create little bundles.

4. Now attach the wire to the frame and next attach a little bundle by wrapping wire tightly around foliage and wreath to secure.

5. Take your second bundle and place it so it covers the stem of the previous bunch. Use the wire to secure it tightly. Repeat this the whole way around, making sure the inside and outside of the ring are covered.

6. When you've covered the wreath, look to see if there are any gaps. Use little stalks and trimming to fill these.

7. To hang your wreath, loop a section of ribbon round the wreath. Hang it in its new home.

8. Stand back and admire your sweet handiwork . . . . then, if you're so inclined, post a proud wee photo on Instagram.

## EARD-FAST *(ADJ),* DEEP-ROOTED IN THE EARTH

Gardens in Scotland have often been used to harness the usefulness of the ground around us. In the inter-war period of the 20th century, Scottish citizens were encouraged to use their gardens and any land available to them to grow vegetables. Gardens were a significant part of the council housing schemes at this time for this very reason, but the density of such housing built in Scotland meant there was less provision for this than in England. Allotments and community gardens were adopted as the solution. And so, by the end of the Second World War, there were 90,000 plots in Scotland.

Now, thanks to popular demand, it can be fairly difficult to get an allotment plot. In 2017, the Greenspace Use and Attitude Survey found that 50% of Scots surveyed said they would like to grow their own produce but couldn't currently do so. Unsurprisingly, the lack of a garden is cited as the main barrier (44% of people asked), followed by a lack of the necessary gardening skills (32%), then those who don't have time (26%) and those who are unable to get an allotment (14%).

The Community Empowerment (Scotland) Act 2015 requires local authorities to make real efforts to facilitate growing produce in the community. So, we can only hope that it will become increasingly easier to grow your own vegetables if you wish to do so.

## CONTEMPORARY CROFTING

A croft is a small plot of ground adjacent to a house and used as a kitchen garden or for pasture by the tenants and/or community. Of course, for centuries, many Scots had little choice but to live off the land via crofts. Most commonly found in the north-west of Scotland, crofters were, and still are, self-sufficient, sharing skills, aptitudes and workloads with members of their families and their wider community.

### THE URBAN CROFT

To tackle the lack of green space for many residents of towns and cities, community groups have magnificently harnessed this ancient way of living, thereby meeting the needs of people who don't have garden access. 'Urban crofts'

continue a community-based tradition in order to address more contemporary issues of diet, isolation and loneliness.

Leith Community Croft is a great example of this. Next to a disused bowling club at the north-east point of Leith Links, the community croft provides a new way of life for the planters – there is always someone weeding, digging and sowing when you walk past. It is truly a heartwarming thing to see. However, establishing such urban crofts isn't always straightforward; unfortunately, not everyone appreciates the time and effort that goes into such a project – or the philosophy behind it. But in an era of individuality, it is invigorating to see people embodying the principles of community and self-sufficiency.

Coorie Bookshelf

*A Scots Dictionary of Nature*
Amanda Thomson

# OH KALE YEAH

So, what veg can we grow here in Scotland? They have seen a resurgence in popularity thanks to the health-food craze, but nutrient-filled anti-glam crops such as kale (or 'kail' in Scots, a generic word for dinner) and beetroot have been signed-up members of the Scottish vegetable patch since before even your great-grandad can remember.

Kale is a brilliant ingredient for seasonal eaters as it is one of the few green vegetables that's more abundant and flavourful during the coldest months of the year. Shetland kale has the honour of being the oldest Scottish local vegetable variety. The poem 'Auld Maunsie's Cro' by Basil R. Anderson, written in Shetland, memorialises the kale:

> Auld Maunsie
> biggit him a Cro
> Ta grow him kale
> fir mutton bro
> Fir Maunsie never
> tocht him hale,
> Withoot sheeps
> shanks an kogs
> o'kale.

## A PLANTIE CRUB

Seeds for Shetland kale aren't sold commercially – more mainstream strains tend to dominate the market – so to acquire some you might have to take a trip to the Shetlands yourself. On Shetland, and many other isles, as you might well know, the relentless wind makes growing anything a challenge! Hence the invention of 'plantie crubs'; these walled enclosures, often circular in shape, shield the vulnerable kale shoots.

Plantie crubs remind me of the formal walled gardens that we associate with castles and large estates. These were also built for the similar purpose of keeping the elements, relatively, at bay from the vegetables – but had the added bonus of safeguarding the ladies' hats as they observed the natural beauty of the gardens. If you have a suitable selection of beachcombed pebbles you could try creating your own little – possibly ornamental – plantie crub as a stony Shetland backdrop for your garden's more delicate plants.

## BEETRAW

Beetroot – 'beetraw' in Scots – first grows in January, and is then in season for most of the year. Treated properly, beetroot is everyone's friend: it goes well with horseradish, mustard, haggis and spices such as cardamom. It grows with a bountiful plumage of nutritious, iron-rich leaves that taste and look similar to rainbow chard. They're usually thrown away, either at the farm or the market, but those stems and leaves are delicious, cooked or raw. Give them a good wash first and then try finely shredding the stalks into a coleslaw and wilt the leaves, and dress with olive oil and lemon.

Another excellent beetroot fact I'll bet you didn't know is that this remarkable root serves as a hangover cure. Betacyanin, the pigment that gives beetroot its colour, is an antioxidant, so the humble beetroot could be the key to beating your hangover. That's because betacyanin speeds up the process of detoxification in your liver.

## QUIT POLLEN MY LEG

Scots love the extravagance and largesse of hosting, but they are also trained from birth to 'eke out every last drop' whenever they can. This means looking to everything present in the domestic environment, from the chickens to blankets, from food in the cupboard to leftovers from last night's dinner to see how these can be used to the best of their ability. Taking on different aspects of the traditional small-holding life – such as keeping bees and chickens as well as maintaining a variety of compost heaps including a wormery – can enable you to adopt this philosophy and become self-sufficient.

Such self-sufficiency is also worth nurturing in the very young. A primary school in Edinburgh enjoyed brief national notoriety when the pecky dynamics of the school chicken coop made headlines. But the real story here is about children learning the skills and sense of responsibility needed to care for their half-dozen chickens, collect their eggs and then sell them – fresh, organic, free range – on a Friday afternoon. It feels good to imagine some of these mini-smallholders growing up to keep backyard chickens in their own coorie homes.

## HONEY FOR MY HONEY

Honey is harvested yearly. In the north of Scotland, bees from small hives (bee-binks) are often taken up in the car to the heather on or around 12th August, a time known as the 'Glorious Twelfth' (in reference to the grouse-shooting season). The heather flowers will have nectar for only four to six days during the entire season, so for beekeepers it's vital not to miss them.

Scottish heather honey has been proved to be as useful as manuka honey and costs a fraction of the price. Scots have used heather honey as a wound treatment for centuries, and dark honeys like that influenced by heather are powerful antioxidants. Local beekeepers who move their hives to the heather often share the necessary equipment to jar up the specifically thick honey, as it is so different after the bees' exposure to heather.

The dry conditions of 2018 meant the heather honey harvest was unfortunately low compared to previous years. My beekeeping friend Andy in Inverness only gleaned five jars compared to the usual 30. This hints at why Scotland's mixed-weather summers are actually ideal for bees! The wet and cooler climate of Scotland ensures the heather can grow – and be pollinated by the bees.

After honey has been harvested, you not only have glorious multipurpose honey, but the substrate of wax, which can be transformed into useful objects. It's a simple by-product of honey production, but still beeswax from the honeycomb (or 'came' in Scots) is sought after for its use in woodworking, beauty products and even quilt making. People have been making beeswax candles in Scotland since the Middle Ages, and if you have ready access to beeswax be sure to use this as a lovely DIY gift option.

Coorie Bookshelf

*The Bees*
Carol Ann Duffy

## A GOOD EGG

Like the primary-school children mentioned above, if you're worried about where your eggs come from, give yourself peace of mind and invest in a chicken coop! It is best for chickens to have plenty of space and a covered area to comply with regulations regarding poultry-based diseases. Unlike bees, chickens definitely need proper access to grass and green spaces. It's possible to keep poultry in smaller spaces but with less grass to eat, they may start to peck at each other instead – which is far from ideal. Chickens usually lay one egg a day, but not if something stressful has happened. This snippet of information might make you reflect on human productivity when under stress! An added bonus is that if you can persevere past the smell, chicken excrement is actually the best manure for increasing levels of nitrogen in your soil.

If you don't keep hens, then keep an eye out for free-range eggs when you are next doing a shop. This ensures the eggs come from chickens that are not confined in battery farms. Organic eggs are ace, too; with their deep, rich yolks, you can tell when eggs are from well-cared-for chickens. Or maybe a friend, neighbour or colleague has hens, and you can trade some eggs for a jar of homemade jam!

If you're on a rural road trip, look out for 'Eggs for Sale' signs as you go. Many people like to sell boxes of fresh local eggs; card payments are not accepted, you simply put your money in the delightfully named honesty box!

**THE COMPOSITION OF COMPOST**
Wormeries and various compost heaps require day-to-day attention; the more frequently they are turned, the better

the compost becomes. Straw (from any livestock you might keep) is added to a specific bin, in which urine can be used to initiate the composting process. This speaks to the Highlands and Islands tradition of keeping a pee bale, as well as using urine in the dyeing of fabric and fibre. Some councils in the UK will provide you with compost bins so you can minimise waste and make the most of your garden – have a wee look and see if your local council is doing this.

Clearly, the practicalities might feel a bit 'icky' to begin with, but compost really can transform your coorie garden – you'll see the difference as soon as springtime blooms. It has extraordinary environ-mental benefits, too, keeping food scraps out of landfill and chemicals out of the earth.

## TUTTI FRUTTI

Scottish royal castles had orchards as early as the 14th century, long before they were grown in country estates. Kitchen gardens and orchards became popular in the 1600s, at a similar time that sugar started to be more widely available in Scotland. The more affluent used sugar as a preservative, producing jams as well as other treats to impress guests. Later, commercially made bottled jams and preserves – such as those produced by John Gray & Co. – were cheaper and more widely available.

Nowadays, the variety of fruit grown in the typical Scottish garden, as well as lemons and oranges, are often made into jams and curds; the latter using the eggs from your own or friendly local chickens, if possible. The nostalgic pleasures of 'pick your own' are a great way to harvest fresh fruit ready for preserve making. Remember to save a good selection of glass jars throughout the year so you're ready to line your cupboards in a truly coorie way when jam season arrives. If you are a keen preserver but struggle to find space for your abundance of vessels and jars, think about putting up some extra shelves, as your homemade produce will make for a lovely display.

Early summer in Scotland will bring you strawberries, blackcurrants, goose-berries and cherries to stock up on.

Those you can't use in your jams and preserves, you can freeze for later – they'll keep for ages and nothing is lovelier than raspberries you picked yourself on a bowl of porridge in the dark days of February.

September marks your last chance to get your hands on home-grown raspberries and wild blackberries but is the perfect time to make the most of the apples available. Surely no one ever tires of the sheer comforting joy that is apple and blackberry crumble – especially when you've spent a sunny afternoon wandering quiet lanes and filling old ice-cream tubs with the fruit of hedgerows?

The addition of a handwritten label and neatly tied cloth lid-cover to your jars of jam, marmalade and chutney will make them beautifully gift-worthy for the festive season or any other occasion. It's heartwarming to receive and even more heartwarming to be the giver of such thrifty, personal and timeless treats, to bring coorie into the homes of friends and family.

If marmalade is your thing, then don't forget that the peel from the oranges you use to make marmalade can be dried out very easily on the top of a radiator and used as fantastic fire starters or kindling. This blows my mind! You can also make delicate candles from clementines by carefully dividing the fruit in two and removing the segments, keeping the pith intact. Once you pour a little oil into the remaining peel, you can light the pith and hey presto, you've made yourself a candle.

# Gran P's raspberry jam

My notoriously hospitable gran is always cooking and baking for all manner of social situations. She makes jams all year round to give to others, and the one that my mouth waters for the most is her raspberry jam. Here I share her trade secrets!

**You will need:**

2kg of raspberries

2kg of sugar (granulated is best)

a selection of jars with well-fitting lids (be sure to sterilise)

waxed circles to seal are handy but not essential

some saucers cooled in the freezer (for your 'setting test')

a jam kettle if you have one

**Method:**

1. Put your raspberries into a large pan or jam kettle (no need to add water).

2. Cook gently until the raspberries are tender and juicy.

3. Add the sugar and stir in until dissolved over a low heat, then increase the heat to a good 'rolling' boil.

4. Test for setting after 5 minutes and continue boiling until the setting point is reached.

5. To do your setting test, put a spot of jam on a cold saucer and draw a spoon across it. When it wrinkles, setting point is reached.

6. Pot the jam in warm sterilised jars. Seal, cover and label. Enjoy!

## BE SEASONAL

The thought of trying to live more seasonally can be very daunting; it's hard to
know where to start. I have found visual-
ising the different times of the year helps.
Season by season, you start to see which
fruit and veg grow at similar times, and it
gets a little easier. I hope my interpretation of a seasonal diary of when different
crops are available in Scotland helps.

## SCOTTISH FRUIT & VEG DIARY

### WINTER

Beetroot, Brussels Sprouts, Cabbage,
Carrots, Chicory, Leeks, Mushrooms,
Potatoes

December – Parsnips, Squash, Turnips,
Apples, Pears

January – Broccoli, Parsnips, Turnips,
Pears

February – Broccoli

### SPRING

Broccoli, Cabbage, Carrots, Chicory,
Mushrooms, Potatoes

March – Brussels Sprouts, Leeks,
Radishes

April – Leeks, Radishes

May – Asparagus, Cauliflower, Lettuce

## SUMMER

Cabbage, Carrots, Cauliflower, Celery, Courgettes, Lettuce, Mushrooms, Onions, Potatoes, Gooseberries, Raspberries, Strawberries

June – Asparagus, Broad Beans, Runner Beans, Tayberries, Rhubarb, Redcurrants

July – Beetroot, Broad Beans, Broccoli, French Beans, Peas (shell), Peas (sugar snap), Runner Beans, Shallots, Blackcurrants, Blueberries, Loganberries, Redcurrants, Tomatoes, Rhubarb

August – Aubergines, Beetroot, Broccoli, French Beans, Peas (shell), Peas (sugar snap), Runner Beans, Shallots, Blackberries, Blueberries

## AUTUMN

Beetroot, Cabbage, Carrots, Celery, Chicory, Leeks, Mushrooms, Parsnips, Potatoes, Apples, Pears

September – Broccoli, Cauliflower, French Beans, Lettuce, Onions, Shallots, Summer Squash, Turnips, Blackberries, Blueberries, Damsons, Plums, Raspberries, Strawberries

October – Broccoli, Brussels Sprouts, Cauliflower, Celeriac, Courgettes, Kale, Lettuce, Onions, Pumpkin, Squash, Elderberries

November – Brussels Sprouts, Chestnuts, Pumpkin, Squash

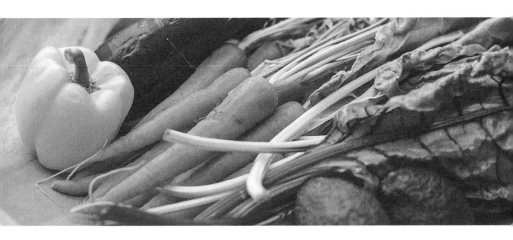

# Home Away From Home

Short stays, time away and
taking Scotland with you

**9**

Scotland is a country with a decidedly human face. It is this personality – the contradictions, flaws, joys, ambiguities and ironies of human life – that makes Scotland such a unique place to visit. The scenic panoramas, the sweeping natural beauty and sense of ruggedness, combined with the hospitality and personable nature of the population, construct the narrative of Scotland as 'home', even if it is only for a short time.

So, when Scots move further afield, as we have historically been prone to do, how does being Scottish manifest itself in different locations around the world? How does coorie work for the Scottish diaspora and for those in a long-distance relationship with Scotland?

# LONG-DISTANCE
# RELATIONSHIPS

You might recognise the names of certain places around the world that are of Scottish origin. It feels quite strange to encounter one of the 21 towns called Glasgow in the USA, which seem so far removed from their namesake city. New Zealand's Dunedin is a reflection of the reach of the Scottish diaspora. The name comes from Dùn Èideann, the Gaelic name for Edinburgh. The planner of the New Zealand city, Charles Kettle, wanted to create his own version of Edinburgh's standout characteristics and so produced a bold 'Romantic' design. But builders struggled to realise Kettle's glorious vision in New Zealand's challenging landscape, and the outcome was streets with a charming mix of the grand and the quirky.

**CLOSER TO HOME**

In the rest of the UK, the romantic ideal of Scotland, historically showcased by the writings of Sir Walter Scott and the frequent visits to Balmoral by Queen Victoria, has proved attractive to many. Queen Victoria inspired aristocratic families to retreat to the Highlands to enjoy the pleasures of game hunting and the rugged landscapes.

None of which was entirely un-problematic. The fact that Scotland was an industrialised, active part of the British Empire was largely ignored. Artists from both sides of the border depicted this vision of the country with romantic images of stags, mountains and castles, often adorned with tartan, thereby offering a visual interpretation of Scott's writings and capitalising on an idealised view of Scotland.

The strength of feeling for this version of the country can be seen in the volume of paintings that depict Scottish landscapes, exhibited in public collections around the world. In Manchester, for example, *Autumn Leaves* by Sir John Everett Millais portrays Scotland as an in-between land, both historical and contemporary, neither summer nor winter. The subjects depicted are neither rich nor poor, perfectly bolstering this vision of Scotland as a utopia where poetic dreams can be explored and constraints such as wealth, social class and urbanisation are mainly overlooked. The Gallery of New South Wales in Australia also holds artworks in its collection that depict Scotland in this romantic fashion. *Rising Mists* by Peter Graham was purchased by the Gallery in 1888; it portrays a Scottish glen adorned with dramatic sunlight, mist – and Highland coos.

Coorie Bookshelf

## *The Outrun*
## Amy Liptrot

*Elsewhere, Home*
Leila Aboulela

## THE AMERICAS

In 2015, I lived in Canada. Studying in Calgary (near the Canadian Rockies rather than on the Isle of Mull) was a transformative experience for me. I definitely found elements of Scottish hospitality in the friendly and polite manner of the Canadians I met. I also found that not only does the name Calgary echo its Scottish heritage, but the physical presence of the place does, too.

**STILL AS A STATUE**
While there, I had a strange encounter with Robert the Bruce. No, not the actual man, but a statue of him – on horseback,

dressed in armour and ready for battle. However, this was not an original statue but an exact bronze replica of the statue situated at the Battle of Bannockburn visitor centre in Stirling, Scotland. As I looked up at the replica king, in front of Alberta University of the Arts, with one of the best views of the city of Calgary before me, I observed Scotland and Canada in a single setting. This seemed incredible given the 4,000 miles between Calgary, Canada and Calgary, Scotland.

I knew that the original statue in Bannockburn was created using the actual measurements of Bruce's skull (rediscovered at Dunfermline Abbey in

1818) and was first unveiled by Queen Elizabeth II in 1964. Eric L. Harvie, a lawyer, philanthropist and the founder of the Glenbow Museum in Calgary, played a significant role in funding the original Robert the Bruce statue at the site of the Battle of Bannockburn. It was at Harvie's insistence that Calgary gained its identical twin statue to demonstrate the connection between Scotland and Canada that Harvie had helped create.

For good and for bad, Scottishness has shaped areas of international culture. So many Scots emigrated by choice or necessity that arguably Scotland's ultimate export has been its people. Burns clubs, St Andrew's Day celebrations and Highland Games are prevalent throughout North America and beyond as a result of Scots continuing their native culture wherever they land. The energy that sees these traditions adapted and flourishing in their new homes reflects the pride in their Scottish heritage that so many of the diaspora feel. It also indicates the numbers of people who are happy to claim this heritage, even if only to join in a party! This passion for ancestral lands has spurred on funding for Scottish film and television. *Outlander*, for example, was filmed in Scotland but has a large American team behind it. It's based, too, on books by American author Diana Gabaldon.

> " Perhaps the greatest of all Scottish exports has been its sons and daughters. Their legacy has left an indelible mark across the globe. "

DR STEPHEN MULLEN
UNIVERSITY OF GLASGOW

**EMPIRE LINES**

Only recently have we begun to acknowledge that Scottish heritage is present in many places around the world because of Scotland's active role in Empire. For a small country, Scotland has played a significant – and sometimes troubling – part in history.

Patterns of emigration have also had a huge impact on American life. The whisky trade boomed in North America, for example, after many travelled across the Atlantic from Scotland and Ireland. The sheer number of Scots who settled in the USA can be seen in the considerable influence that Gaelic culture had on language and music. Many church services were conducted in Gaelic; the United Presbyterian Church of Boston did so until the late 1900s.

## HAME AWA FAE HAME

But, back to our contemporary lives, what if you have a short time to experience as much of Scotland as possible? How do you source yourself that elusive, authentic experience? If you can, finding a unique place to stay makes all the difference; individuality definitely creates homely vibes. And it's true that us Scots love to bring along our favourite touches to personalise our time away, such as a pair of comfy baffies or even a selection of favourite teabags.

## WOODEN LODGES OR CABINS

These make for perfect Scottish get-aways, which is surely why there are so many to choose from. A small cosy space, with great views of mountains or wild vistas, allows you to connect with the outside while chilling inside. Micro cabins are a decidedly coorie option, and if you can get your hands on some local produce to sustain you throughout your trip then you are set for a calm and simple outdoorsy stay.

## A BOTHY LIFE

If you are looking for a take-no-prisoners place to stay, one that will connect you both to the land and history of Scotland, then it has to be a bothy. The experience of bothying is best described as 'camping without a tent'. Historically used solely by farmers as respite or shelter from rough weather, bothies are rustic buildings that can be found across rural Scotland and which now serve as basic accommodation for anyone.

Staying in a bothy is a sublime experience that offers a mirror into how people have lived for hundreds of years. Nowadays bothies are usually left unlocked and open to anyone; unavoidably they encompass a very inclusive – and trusting – community vibe. When visiting, assume that there will be scarce or no facilities. Basic is the word, although

most kind souls will leave a tin of baked beans, a jar of coffee or a box of matches for the next resident as a pay-it-forward salute. As stated on the Mountain Bothies Association website, 'all comforts have to be carried in'.

**The MBA Bothy Code**
- Respect the Bothy
- Respect Other Users
- Respect the Surroundings
- Respect Agreement with the Estate
- Respect the Restriction on Numbers

Bothies are situated directly in the landscape, and some are in absolutely stunning locations, such as 'The Lookout'

(*Rubha Hunish*), which is a former coast-guard watch station in northern Skye. If you're lucky, it makes for an amazing place from which to spot whales!

Built into the Mangersta cliffs in the parish of Uig on the west coast of the Isle of Lewis, the Eagles' Nest (Mangersta bothy) exudes a feeling of reflection and significance in its situation and its creation. The bothy literally sits on the cusp of the Atlantic, and on a clear day this is a prospect with views of St Kilda, the most westerly and isolated part of Scotland.

Unlike many, this bothy was built by John and Lorna Norgrove with the specific intention of housing travellers for a night or two. This was 30 years ago, before the resurgence of bothy popularity. Now the Eagles' Nest is one of the most sought-after bothy retreats in Scotland, and to stay there you need to request a date via the Linda Norgrove Foundation. Like all bothies, it offers free accommodation, but the foundation always welcomes any donations.

**I DO LIKE TO BE BESIDE . . .**

Before travelling abroad became as straightforward as hopping on a plane, holidaymakers flocked to British seaside towns and resorts for some time in the sun, even if it was only a daytrip and a paddle in the sea rather than a fortnight under a beach umbrella. Scotland was no different, if you can believe it. Scottish beaches were so popular in the Victorian era that it makes me wonder if the weather was much warmer then! Or if now we have been spoiled by experiencing more exotic climates in much more

minimal outfits than the Victorians might have deemed proper.

Towns such as St Andrews and North Berwick are so gloriously situated and unspoiled in their coorie charms that they still remain top destinations for weekend breakers and holidaymakers. Though the grand and exuberant mansions of the past are now often divided into smaller homes, you can still enjoy magnificent views of the coastline – and some delightfully traditional holiday pastimes such as pitch and putt and ice-cream parlours – even if the weather is too blustery for a sunbathe.

For a more secluded and faraway experience, Luskentyre beach on the Isle of Harris is heralded as one of the best beaches in the world. Its peerless sands and deep turquoise waters are magical; explore a little further and find equally breathtaking vistas of your own.

Coorie Bookshelf

*Overlander*
Alan Brown

**THE WATER OF LIFE**

The various restorative and invigorating pleasures of water have always played a vital role in Scottish getaways. For example, the late 19th century saw a huge boom in the popularity of hydropathic hotels, many of which are still around today.[i] Although the practice of hydro-pathy – the use of water as pain relief or as a cure for ailments – has evolved over the years, the practice of healing and relaxation techniques in close proximity to water is still popular whether one is a resident of or visitor to Scotland.

The joy of attending a yoga session at Drift café near North Berwick on a cliff looking out to the Firth of Forth, indulg-ing in a spa weekend fuelled with fresh spring water at a rural 'Hydro', or initiating your own hydropathy where you live – perhaps at the traditional Turkish Baths at Portobello – is an accessible one which promises positive, long-lasting benefits.

Proximity to one of the thousands of Scottish freshwater lochs also offers a fabulous way for everyone to interact with the environment and water. As a rule of thumb, the further north you go, the more lochs you'll find to explore – and there are thousands of them. Some are havens of watery tranquillity, perfect for spotting Scottish wildlife such as ospreys; others you might like to explore either by wild swimming, canoeing or walking – or perhaps take the less sporty option of a steamship cruise on Loch Katrine.

> We twa hae paidl'd
> i' the burn,
> Frae mornin' sun
> till dine;
> But seas between
> us braid hae roar'd
> Sin auld lang syne.

**ROBERT BURNS**

## BY LOCH, RIVER AND SEA

This verse from 'Auld Lang Syne' evokes the deep attachment that so many people the world over have to the homeland of Burns. It hints that an affinity with Scotland also implies a connection to the land and sea. The River Tay (*Tatha*) flows from the stunning expanse of Loch Tay to the North Sea, linking the remote splendour of the Highlands to the rest of the world. In my mind it embodies the wild spaces in which you might paddle even if you then leave Scotland to travel to places far away. From Kenmore to Dundee, there are so many lochside and riverside places that will welcome you with that gorgeous combination of homely cosy vibes and contemporary Scottish design and hospitality.

If you want somewhere to call a home away from home, with plentiful Scottish comforts built in, the Steading, a luxury B&B, is a fantastic fusion of old and new. Located just outside of Aberfeldy, a charming market town on the banks of the River Tay, you'll find tartan touches, locally sourced antiquarian objects and bright clean rooms that showcase epic views of snow-capped mountains and rugged landscapes through frame-like windows. You can't beat such personable hosts and delectable breakfasts, as well as the chance to sit outside, snuggled in a woollen blanket, coffee in hand to survey the scenery of Perthshire.

Along the river, Grandtully (pronounced without the 'd') sits on the south bank of the Tay, opposite the village of Strathtay. The Grandtully Hotel offers a luxury home-from-home experience, fuelled by the same passions for local food and the warm welcome of genuine hospitality as its founders brought to bear at Ballintaggart Farm. Each of the hotel's eight bedrooms is boldly unique, mixing vibrant colours and fixtures with more homely traditional touches. The hotel features a phenomenal restaurant and bar, as well as little nooks in which to relax and maybe sip a glass of whisky if the moment strikes you. Special spaces such as the Grandtully Hotel, which are designed and curated with such thoughtful intentionality, sum up all the attributes of a lived experience that might best showcase contemporary Scotland.

## WHEREVER YOU ARE

Near or far, Scotland can be perceived in many different ways. Pinpointing what coorie means to you will help determine what you look for in a Scottish getaway as well as what you hold dear if you leave Scotland. Abstracted Scottish culture found around the world feels distant to the reality of living in a 21st-century Scotland, but cosiness, hospitality and connecting with those who share your enthusiasm for Scotland all have the power to transport you right back home.

So, what does coorie look like in this context of a long-distance relationship? Whenever I'm away, I always feel most like I'm at home when the light is a certain way – dim and dreich outside and with that warm light inside. It evokes a feeling that is so homely, cosy and familiar. I've found that a (growing) collection of woollen blankets, whether super-luxe, vintage or homemade, are great keepsakes to embody Scottishness wherever in the world you may be living. On cool, damp nights it's heavenly to curl up on the couch with them, and possibly a canine companion or two. Not as long lasting, but when I visit faraway Scottish friends, they often ask me to smuggle in rations of Irn Bru, all the permutations of Tunnocks teatime snacks, blocks of tablet and other national treasures such as 'proper porridge oats', for delicious reminders of Scotland.

# Granny Menzies' tablet

**Below is Ciara's famed family recipe for delectable tablet. It's a peerless sweet comfort wherever you go!**

**You will need:**
900g caster sugar
a large tin of condensed milk
85g butter (chopped into pieces)
one cup of milk

**Method:**
1. Place all ingredients in a pan on a very low heat till completely dissolved. It's important to take this stage very slowly.
2. Increase the heat until the mixture boils while stirring very frequently then reduce the heat to a gentle boil.
3. Stir on and off until the mixture is gloppily thick and light brown.
4. You can add any additional flavours at this stage – though traditionalists might frown at such fancy goings-on.
5. Whisk or beat off the heat until thick and then pour into a greased Swiss roll tin or baking tray.
6. Leave to cool. When it's cool but still soft, cut into squares.
7. Once your tablet is completely cool, serve and enjoy.
8. If there's any left, store in an airtight tin.

A SWEET COORIE GIFT: You can always put some squares into decorative little bags or tubs, and you'll find that tablet makes a very tasty present.

# Coorie Looking Forward

# 10

## An evolution

## HOW WILL SCOTTISH LIVING LOOK IN YEARS TO COME?

Some people have a tongue-in-cheek approach to Scotland's future. With increasing temperatures around the globe, more people might be attracted to Scotland because of its relatively milder climate, which in turn could mean that Glasgow and Edinburgh fuse into a mega city! There are even those who speculate that insect protein in the form of midge haggis could become part of our mainstream diet. Who knows?

### A RETURN TO THE PAST?

There are a few elements of domestic living that we *can* expect to become increasingly popular. Technology will continue to be commonplace in all areas of the home – underfloor heating, for example, is a popular choice for developers seeking a sleek, minimal aesthetic and an eco-friendly alternative. It has been predicted, too, that in the next five years, home-charging stations for electric cars will become commonplace in Scottish houses – reflecting the need to adapt to environmental factors and the fossil-fuel crisis.[i] Likewise, with its blustery, watery landscapes, Scotland enjoys an abundance of renewable energy sources with which it can lead the shift to a clean energy future.

As the population increases, new-build homes will most likely become smaller as available space decreases – something we can already see happening in densely packed areas such as Leith. This pressure on resources particularly in urban environments hints that life will definitely get cosier whether we like it or not! Clever furniture will continue to offer solutions to spatial limitations and – along with imaginative design and a sensibility that encourages adaptability – will be invaluable as people seek out more multipurpose rooms in their homes, and in their outdoor spaces, too.

For example, sheds and summer houses, used for activities other than potting plants and storing bikes, are on the rise. Chic sheds that are enjoyed as home offices, retreats from a noisy world or as playrooms for lucky children are very coorie illustrations of this.

It's intriguing how in an age dominated by technology and science some people are taking a fresh look at our ancestors' lifestyles to find happiness, healthier alternatives and effective ways of living. Our homes are becoming more multipurpose and relaxed in how we allocate function to different areas of the home. In a statistic that's close to my heart, with an estimated 69% of us finding ourselves – whether at leisure

or at work – at a laptop, with no office desk or chair, the need for spaces that cater to all kinds of activities has become paramount.[ii]

## AN EVOLVING AESTHETIC

Scots have taken plenty of first steps into the unknown, especially when it comes to the designer's mindset of enterprise, innovation and imagination. While preserving the brilliance of historical design and architecture, contemporary practices are initiating fresh takes on residential Scotland. Even though many aspects of a typical home in Scotland can feel conservative on a design level, a lot of design innovations made by Scots have a perhaps unexpected hint of the daring.

A great example of this is the work of GRAS – a design practice, part of the established conservation firm Groves-Raines Architects Ltd – which seeks to deliver progressive and sustainable work in a responsive approach. By not conforming to style or trends, projects push the boundaries of what is usually considered as Scottish architecture and design. This seems to encompass the direction visual innovation is taking in Scotland. As Scottish identity has evolved and become more multifaceted over the years, so, too, will Scottish design.

## SO, WHAT'S NEXT FOR SCOTLAND?

Unlike previous generations, we now have online access to unlimited design ideas and materials – all of which can contribute to creativity. (Of course the opposite is also true: innovators of the past perhaps got a lot more done because there was no siren call of the internet and its time-wasting temptations!) For example, we now have the power to seek inspiration, consult our peers and experts alike, then custom design our own properties online and schedule the construction not too soon after. All these elements – however modest or ambitious – of adjusting our living spaces to suit our own vision, lifestyle and priorities can be done more quickly, with more choice and more options. Peeking through a stranger's window for inspiration can still be a guilty pleasure, but the virtual possibilities of such secret insights are boundless now that 'kitchen envy' is an Instagram hashtag.

In the midst of what might be felt as information overload, originality is – and will become increasingly so – more important than ever. This desire for the

unique and the original, something that feels true to you, extends not only to finding and choosing your actual home but also to how you style it.

*Architectural Digest*'s take on this is that the hunger for signifiers of individuality will fuel an international boom in the antiques industry, as folk crave one-of-a-kind pieces for their home. In Scotland this isn't huge news, as we love a charity-shop find, a flea-market bargain and aren't averse to a Sunday morning spent at our local boot fair. Away from the more obviously vintage, I do believe this hints at genuinely good news for grassroots creatives, those entrepreneurs who make one-offs for a living.

**The contemporary craft movement** is beyond popular. Even among hobbyists, there's a boom in 20-somethings tuning into the joys of knitting, jewellery making, quilting, bookbinding, penmanship and macramé. Connecting with the Scottish love for upcycling, people feel inspired to craft decorative elements to individualise their homes, to create spaces lovely to live in. So many of us are signed up to the benefits of an edited, decluttered life. But minimalism doesn't have to be stark or cold; with home-grown and home-spun touches of coorie, your home will soon warm up and become cosy.

Some aspects of our homes might reflect the way we make a living – or the ways in which others once worked in the environments we now inhabit. Metallic objects speak to an industrial turn in interiors, where spaces that used to be factories or warehouses are repurposed for residential use. In other environments, busts of deer, mounted antlers and touches of foliage can reflect the ancient practice of working the land.

But what might this aesthetic look like going forward? Is it appropriate to enjoy such aesthetics when they are so disconnected from the way many of us live now? Well, I'd argue yes. It feels there is a resurgence in noticing and learning from what our ancestors did before us, whether this is in terms of sustainable living or in vocational choices. For example, when I spoke to young game-keepers, I realised they spend most of their time practising – and evolving – traditions many of us wouldn't be aware still exist. This is reflected in the spe-cialist equipment found throughout their living spaces, as well as memorandums of their achievements in their careers. So, with an expanding knowledge of wildlife, animal husbandry and the wider ecosys-tem, these ways of life can be sustained and made newly meaningful, developing the heritage of Scotland as we go.

**TARTAN CHIC**

Okay, let's be real. To the outside world tartan signifies a key element of that heritage – and no one can deny the international reverence that tartan enjoys or the cloth's value as an expression of Scotland's history and identity.

But the truth is that not every Scot has tartan in their home. In fact, probably very few do – certainly not in the ostentatious fashion of old. But tartan's status as a symbol of Scotland's history and its powerful identity are surely deserved. The ways the colours of different tartans reflect the natural dyes found in Scotland are uniquely beautiful.

Coorie Bookshelf

*A Drunk Man Looks at the Thistle*
Hugh MacDiarmid

## REFLECTED IN NATURE

Using nature as a source of inspiration for colour and form is a practice that extends beyond tartan. Scottish creatives and makers, as they offer a vast range of alternatives to the high street, reflect the natural landscapes, seascapes and skyscapes of Scotland in distinctive homewares and cosy clothing. Some of the products might look very different to traditional tartan and tweed, but still you can see vibrant echoes of a contemporary Scotland in them.

**Emily Millichip** has worked as an artist in Edinburgh since 2008, and she has been challenging what Scottish fashion and textiles look like since the get-go – including international collaborations with an indigenous-owned design practice in Australia. With her shoppers, clutches and purses in bright neons and tropical prints, which don't obviously scream Scotland, she has made her playful, punkish brand.

Paradise Palms in Edinburgh is a favourite for Emily's pop-up shop, as the bar's interior seamlessly matches the colours and subversive twists of her creations. However, when exploring Emily's recent interior work, it is crystal clear that living right on the coast in Portobello has inspired fresh colour choices and decorative touches.

## LOUNGING ABOUT

The clothes we wear indoors are constantly shifting, too, with the style of loungewear evolving to the point where beautiful knitted pieces fuse with urban shapes such as trackies. (Tracksuit bottoms are not a garment generally known for their effortless cool.) This intersection marks a place where Scotland's unique textile heritage becomes fused with more dynamic, urban styles of clothing. As sportswear advances in terms of its cut, fabric and patterning to become much more accepted outside of the football pitch, yoga studio, race track or gym, this development in wearability changes the face of cosy.

**Atelier E.B** is a fine example of a fashion label that challenges, destabilises and critiques with its idiosyncratic designs. The company consists of designer Beca Lipscombe and the artist Lucy McKenzie, who strive to bring products that are uniquely category-defying *and* sustainable straight to the customer. Their garments speak of urban landscapes as well as hinting at rural ones, specifically through the use of wool. The Calton sweatshirt, for example, includes bold visuals of a well-known landmark in Scotland's capital. Their neoclassical nylon tracksuits recognise the democratic anonymity of the ubiquitous tracksuit but also (so they say!) the power of its sexual charge.

These playful, knowing takes on Scottish identity indicate how, as many of us inhabit more highly populated areas, it is inevitable that the environments from which we gain our inspiration may change. The Scottish passion for rolling hills, snowy mountains, panoramic glens and breathtaking beaches won't disappear, but this love will join with more urban, 21st-century influences to colour and shape interior and personal design.

## GOING GREEN

As the human race faces the biggest threat of extinction it has ever experienced – environmental breakdown and climate change – efforts are made to source and create sustainable sources of energy for our homes. It is crucial now – more than ever before – to take purposeful steps to 'go green' to ensure the elements of coorie that come from our natural surroundings in Scotland are not lost or irredeemably damaged.

**WOOL AND WHISKY**

It is self-evident that climate change means the weather will become more erratic and unreliable, putting livestock and plants at risk. Diapensia, Norwegian mugwort, and particularly cloudberry, for example, which we know have grown here since at least 3650 BCE could be wiped out thanks to lack of snowfall.

In 2019, farms in the north of Scotland lost up to 50 lambs after the lambing season began early because of misleadingly warm weather, which was followed by a dangerous drop in temperature – fatal for the newborn lambs not yet strong enough to withstand the cold. As is often the case, those with close, active connections to the earth are the most directly impacted by – and the first to notice – the encroaching drama of catastrophe.

With rising summer temperatures jeopardising crops such as wheat, the Scottish whisky industry could be at risk, too. Yes, on the plus side, higher temperatures could see barley crop yields remaining steady and actually rising across Scotland. On the other hand, some yields decreased in areas such as the south-west of Scotland because of soil saturation. Increased rainfall doesn't automatically mean more 'water of life'. The increasing risk of floods, especially from rivers, will inevitably have a negative impact on facilities and crops located nearby.

**IN A THRANTLE HOLE**

They might have been a precursor of landfill, but we have come a long way from the use of 'thrantle holes', a Scots term for a pit dug into the earth, located near a home where people discarded all their household waste that couldn't be eaten by animals. The relentless escalation of our modern landfill habits means, though, that the prospect of the impact of climate change on all our lives – and those of generations to come – is bleak, but it's a reality that must be faced.

My sense is that a true understanding of what we stand to lose will catalyse a movement of change that has the potential to save the things we hold dear – and to transform our approach to life to create a more sustainable future.

By putting in the effort to change our ways, we can make a difference for ourselves, the environment and future generations. The following are some great ways to get started.

1. **Eat in tune with the seasons.** This will help cut down on carbon emissions and prevent food shortages as more food is locally produced and consumed.

2. **Discover the joys of your native land.** Take holidays in such a way that you don't need to fly. Be radical; take a ferry, catch a bus or a train, share a car! This will make a huge difference to the amount of fuel you use.

3. **Be rigorously conscious about what you buy, what materials you use and what you throw away.** This will help to preserve the landscapes and ecosystems we know and love.

> "When I was a child, people sat around the kitchen table and told their stories. We don't do that so much anymore. Sitting around the table telling stories is not just a way of passing time. It is the way the wisdom gets passed along. Despite the awesome powers of technology many of us still do not live very well. We may need to listen to one another's stories again."

DR RACHEL NAOMI REMEN, KITCHEN TABLE WISDOM

## A KITCHEN-TABLE APPROACH

Having a blether around the kitchen table can often be the best medicine for any of life's woes and worries.

There is a wisdom in these conversations that can't be found anywhere else. Those informal, intimate tables at the heart of the home are where lively chatter, interruptions, disagreements, heartfelt stories, bad jokes and the sense of peace that comes from an airing of one's quandaries come together. It's an environment where everyone can participate in thoughtful, enjoyable discussion in a way that seems to transcend boundaries, hinting that a propensity for such interactions is virtually hardwired into our DNA.

This act of sitting together around a kitchen table is essential to a coorie home. It's a social interaction idiom that is now moving beyond the home into other areas of life.

The kitchen-table model in business contexts draws on the energy of sitting side by side in a communal living space to generate rambunctious but productive discussions. It's an innovation that has seen great success thus far, offering a more democratic take on the concept of 'holding the room'. And as start-ups and community-based projects pop up more and more, larger organisations are also taking on board those people-centred strategies which offer a more personable approach. From generating ideas to engaging team members in new processes, the kitchen table model is likely to bring a homely – but dynamic, egalitarian and rigorous – essence to many environments in the future.

**A coorie take on the ground rules of kitchen table communication.**

1. **A jargon-free environment** helps all feel welcome in the conversation.

2. **Comfortable disagreement** is good. The idea is that the 'kitchen table' is a space for clarification and healthy debate in the name of creativity and productivity.

3. **As in a social setting**, participants are more honest in a relaxed environment; taking turns to interrupt makes the conversation stronger and culls irrelevant ideas.

4. **Anywhere can be a good spot** for your 'kitchen table'. The beach, the park, a café . . . but perhaps it's best located where you'll not disturb anyone or be overheard.

# THE NEXT CHAPTER

Looking forward, the longevity of the concept and practice of coorie depends on us all working to improve everyone's wellbeing. If coorie is to thrive, then it needs to feel relevant and worthwhile to the next generation of Scots. Thankfully, projects have been initiated that bring coorie alive – through the channels of music and literature – for young children and families.

## COORIE DOON

In 2015, Enterprise Music Scotland began the Coorie Doon project in Edinburgh. A team of a composer, poet and musicians work with parents to make the 'gifts'; together they create songs that emulate the intimacy and security that coorie entails, but which is often hard to find when going through tough situations with children. That first project helped foster wellbeing in families across the north of the city.

The second Coorie Doon was held at the children's hospice, Rachel House. The most recent project was held at the start of 2019 at the Neonatal Unit at the Royal Hospital for Children in Glasgow. Here they found that music enables healing as well as community. The projects achieve both by alleviating some stress in families with prematurely born babies by composing songs for their children, creating another gift to take home alongside their child.

> Literature penetrates and shapes human thought. It transforms people's mentality, alters the way they think, and can, in certain circumstances, shape their identity . . . It is the principal gateway through which questions of value are internalised, articulated, and clarified.[iii]

FRANK FUREDI, SOCIOLOGIST

# WORDS OF TRANSFORMATION

Literature has long since developed in step with the cultural life of Scotland – from John Barbour, writing Scots poems in the 14th century, through Robert Louis Stevenson's epic adventures to Dame Carol Ann Duffy, who addresses gender, love and oppression in her poetry. And you'd hope that with literature being so integral to the Scottish identity that this wouldn't change – rather that it would flourish and adapt as the demographic of Scotland shifts, reflecting a contemporary diversity of voices and telling stories we all need to hear.

## BEDTIME STORIES

A survey by Littlewoods found that two thirds of children in the UK aren't read bedtime stories. This might lead to a more distant relationship with the pleasures of reading, as well as having a negative impact on vocabulary and comprehension skills. Since this finding, the Scottish Government has acknowledged that two of the most important things for a positive upbringing are language and community.

So, what can be done to make sure books – in all their myriad forms – stay present in the Scottish home? Thankfully, in early 2019, a school in north Edinburgh started a first of its kind coorie-in club that has potential to spread wings throughout Scotland and beyond in years to come. The simple idea at the club's core is to make sure every child has access to bedtime stories – a way to mark the end of each day that's comforting, entertaining and educational in the broadest sense. If their parent or carer can't do this physically, Hermitage Park Primary can – by way of their online collection that includes stories read by parents, teachers and even actor Elaine C. Smith. The coorie-in club also runs a get-together every week when pupils and parents can coorie-in for a wee read, uninterrupted by life's sometimes more pressing demands.

Coorie Bookshelf

*Colin and Lee, Carrot and Pea*
Morag Hood

## A BOOK TO LISTEN TO

For adults seeking coorie wellbeing in bookish form, the benefits of the bedtime story are ones we can all reap. Tuning into an audio book can reconnect us with those soothing childhood feelings we associate with hearing someone read to us. Audio books possess an intimacy that speaks directly to our imaginations, heightening our sense of empathy, alleviating stress and helping us to bring a fresh coherence to the world. They enable us to access books that might feel too daunting to 'read' on our own and are a heaven-sent respite for tired eyes. And the beauty of audio is that it's so easy as to be almost effortless – a great addition to any coorie bookshelf.

# COORIE LOOKING FORWARD

The word 'coorie' – with its somewhat disputed meanings of to stoop, bend, snuggle, nestle or to embrace – has been used since the 1700s. This feels like a fitting metaphor for Scottish homes and hospitality, as you might often find yourself entering them to gain respite from harsh conditions, to seek shelter and warmth, like a close hug with a dear friend.

But the etymology of coorie is somewhat complex. Prior to 1700, in the *Dictionary of the Older Scottish Tongue*, coorie is listed as a noun: it's given as a name for the stables of the royal household, originating from the French 'écurie'. In the Scots leid (language), coorie's meanings have been many and various.

'Còsagach' is the Gaelic translation of coorie, and it holds its own meanings that differ from the more recent reading of the word 'coorie'. A more fitting Gaelic equivalent might be the word 'seasgair', an adjective that describes being at ease, snug, warm and comfortable.

**The meaning of coorie** has grown in recent years from a cosy embrace to a term that describes the best of contemporary living in Scotland. Yes, this perhaps marks an Insta-era interpretation of the word – a Scottish alternative to hygge – but when I think of coorie, it has a greater resonance than simply a Scottish aesthetic. To me, coorie describes the way Scots have often, out of choice and necessity, cultivated a deep connection to the earth and the Scottish landscape in all its diversity, from those Iron Age Scots who used incredible resourcefulness to build shelters atop lochs – as seen at the crannogs at Loch Tay – to city-dwelling folk working whatever land they can so as to grow food to provide for their families and the wider local community.

Coorie unites the open-hearted ethos of Scottish hospitality that welcomes anyone in, it drives people to contribute what they can – whether practical, emotional or financial – to others in need, and it seeks to allow the same opportunities to all. Initiatives, from the grassroots coorie-in club to the political commitment to free university tuition for Scottish citizens, all promote a strong desire to nurture the minds of the future, while at the same time conserving and progressing Scotland's uniquely rich culture. Organisations such as the Corbenic Camphill Community and Cranhill Development Trust that combine community and sustainability with an awareness of their geographical settings are striving to move forward in such a way. As are creative-led initiatives like Fóram of Porteous's Studio where local food and company is celebrated equally.

**I imagine coorie** as an affinity between the land, our environment and its people, a union so deep and pleasingly entrenched that Scottish design, architecture and lifestyle have always drawn from it and will continue to do so for many years to come. Coorie is no longer a word of the past and, as it continues to catch the eye of the world, through technology, design and literature, I hope you will be inspired to think about what it means to you and how you can weave it into your life and your coorie home.

Coorie Bookshelf

*The Living Mountain*
Nan Shepherd, audiobook read by Tilda Swinton

# THE COORIE HOME BOOKSHELF

## 1. WHERE D'YOU STAY?
*Findings* by Kathleen Jamie
*Red Dust Road* by Jackie Kay

## 2. WHICH BUZZER?
*A Sense of Place* by Joan Eardley
*Katie Morag's Island Stories* by Mairi Hedderwick

## 3. SHARING'S CARING
*His Bloody Project* by Graeme Macrae Burnet
*Tribes of Glasgow* by Stephen Millar

## 4. THAT'S A BIT NAFF
*Made in Scotland* by Billy Connolly
*The Scottish Nation* by Tom Devine

## 5. AW THAT CLUTTER
*The Cone Gatherers* by Robin Jenkins
*Landing Light* by Don Paterson

## 6. DRESSING GOWN OR HOUSECOAT?
*The Secret Life of Tartan* by Vixy Rae
*The Diary of a Bookseller* by Shaun Bythell

## 7. YOU'LL HAVE HAD YOUR TEA
*Scots Cooking: The Best Traditional and Contemporary Scottish Recipes* by Sue Lawrence
*Morvern Callar* by Alan Warner

## 8. A GID BIT OF FRESH AIR
*A Scots Dictionary of Nature* by Amanda Thomson
*The Bees* by Carol Ann Duffy

## 9. HOME AWAY FROM HOME
*The Outrun* by Amy Liptrot
*Elsewhere, Home* by Leila Aboulela
*Overlander* by Alan Brown

## 10. COORIE LOOKING FORWARD
*A Drunk Man Looks at the Thistle* by Hugh MacDiarmid
*Colin and Lee, Carrot and Pea* by Morag Hood
*The Living Mountain* by Nan Shepherd – audiobook read by Tilda Swinton

"Story is really important in Scotland: we are a small country with long dark winters and the traditions of sitting around a fire sharing stories to pass the time are deeply ingrained.

**PHILIPPA COCHRANE, SCOTTISH BOOK TRUST**

# IMAGE CREDITS

p13  Beth Pearson
p15  The Glue Factory/Agile City CIC
p17, top  David McClure Estate/The Scottish Gallery (photo)
p19, 20  Social Bite
p21, 23  Fingal
p45, bottom  Beth Pearson
p67, top & left  Melody Joy Co.
p67, right  Amelia Claudia Photography
p69  Neill Whiteside of DreamCapture
p97, p98 (bottom)  Andrew Pyott/Beth Pearson (photo)
p100, top & right  BeSeated/Ellie Morag (photo)
p100, left  BeSeated/Paul Cowan (photo)
p102  David Cass 2019 (www.davidcass.art)
p122  Katie Rose Johnston
p125  Juli Bolaños-Durman
p135  Cloh/Harrison Reid (photographeverything.net)
p136, 137  Ruth Mitchell
p185  Robin & Lindsay Burley/Beth Pearson (photo)

# PHOTO LOCATIONS

p54, 55, 58, 59  Corbenic Camphill Community, Dunkeld
p70, 79 (bottom)  Hot Box, Taymouth Marina, Kenmore
p83, 86, 90, 94, 95, 106  The Steading B&B, Aberfeldy
p84  Crannog Centre, Aberfeldy
p107  Highland Safaris Café
p108, 109, 119, 120, 212, 214  Grandtully Hotel, Perthshire
p154  Ballintaggart Farm, Perthshire
p117, 191  Pyrus Botanicals, Edinburgh
p215, 219  Mo Dhachaidh Cottage, Colonsay

# PROP CREDITS

p65  Twice Upon a Chair
p88, 96, 227  Eoghann Menzies of Menzies Design
p132, 139, 146, 198  Araminta Campbell
p140, 143, 145  Rosie Sugden Cashmere
p151, 152  Great Glen Charcuterie
p167, 202, 203  Stellar Health
p231  Murray Hogarth
p239  Aizle Band

# NOTES

2. WHICH BUZZER?
i  MacInnes, R. 'Rubblemania': Ethic and Aesthetic in Scottish Architecture. *Journal of Design History*, vol. 9, no. 3, 1996, pp. 137–151.
ii  www.heraldscotland.com/news/16079158.return-of-the-good-life-the-new-craze-for-front-garden-allotments/
iii  Ibid.
iv  Curl, Angela, et al. 'Physical and Mental Health Outcomes Following Housing Improvements: Evidence from the GoWell Study.' *Journal of Epidemiology and Community Health*, vol. 69, no. 1, 2015, pp. 12–19.
v  Provided by Dualchas Building Design, Skye.

3. SHARING'S CARING
i  Pacione, M., 'Housing Policies in Glasgow since 1880.' *Geographical Review*, Vol. 69, No. 4, 1979, pp. 395–412.
ii  Gazeley, I and Newell, A., *The First World War and Working Class Food Consumption in Britain*. Discussion Paper, IZA, 2010.
iii  Quoted by Brooks, C., Church of Scotland.
iv  Dunbar, R. (2017). 'Breaking Bread: the Functions of Social Eating'. *Adaptive Human Behavior and Physiology*, vol. 3, no. 3, pp. 198–211.

4. THAT'S A BIT NAFF
i  Maudlin, D. 'The Legend of Brigadoon: Architecture, Identity and Choice in the Scottish Highlands.' *Traditional Dwellings and Settlements Review*, vol. 20, no. 2, 2009, pp. 45–57.

6. DRESSING GOWN OR HOUSECOAT?
i  www.thewoolroom.com/blog/why-wool/
ii  Lucas, P., *A Case for Bare Feet*, www.barefooters.org/wp-content/uploads/2015/03/A-Case-for-Bare-Feet.pdf

9. HOME AWAY FROM HOME
i  Bradley, J., Dupree, M. and Durie, A. 'Taking the Water-Cure: The Hydropathic Movement in Scotland, 1840–1940', *Business and Economic History*, vol. 26, no. 2, pp. 426–437.

10. COORIE LOOKING FORWARD
i  www.axa.co.uk/home-insurance/tips-and-guides/homes-of-the-future/
ii  Ibid.
iii  Quoted in *Life in Future Scotland: Growing Up*, (6 March 2018), The Scottish Parliament.

# A HUGE THANK YOU TO . . .

My friends and family for being there throughout this writing experience. Mum and Dad, your love and support has been fantastic; I couldn't have done it without you.

Ciara and all of the Menzies clan who went above and beyond to help create this book. Without you, *The Coorie Home* wouldn't be what it is today!

The Pyotts for having me to stay and for your insight into living sustainably.

Jay for sharing your experience of narrowboat living and to Catriona for introducing us.

Gran and Grandad Pearson for all your insight.

Everyone at Custom Lane, especially Ruth, Roisin and Juli, who were so helpful and wonderful.

Jean, who pointed me in the right direction with my textiles research.

The Glasgow-based creatives, who were so lovely to work with.

Emily, Richard, Peter, Namon and Eoghann for your insight into all things furniture and custom homes.

Jack and Eilidh at Porteous's Studio, Fiona at the Fingal, the team at the Grandtully Hotel and Sarah-Jane, who introduced me to such glorious homes away from homes.

The team at the Social Bite Village, the Camphill Corbenic Community team and the Cranhill Development Trust for allowing me to witness the epic work you do.

Everyone who let Ciara and me into your homes to nosy around and take photos. Visiting your living spaces was a joy!

Everyone who took time to reply to my questions: I really, really appreciate your generosity.

And to the team at Black & White Publishing for making *The Coorie Home* happen – I can't thank you enough!

**BETH PEARSON** is an award-winning graduate of the Glasgow School of Art. She has worked on pre-production of the drama series *Outlander* and at *The Scottish Gallery*, the oldest art gallery in Scotland. Beth is captivated by Scotland's history and culture and says, 'By visiting craftspeople from all round Scotland, I became truly immersed in the contemporary Scottish home. What inspired me the most was how the variety of work I witnessed was united in its love of local landscapes and bringing the outside in.' *The Coorie Home* is Beth's first book. You can find her at @bpearson1995

Originally from the wild Highlands, **CIARA MENZIES** is a photographer and visual storyteller, whose keenness to discover new perspectives has led her around the world. Everyday moments and grand, life-changing ones make the most sense to Ciara in photographs and this, along with her deep love for colour and texture, defines each visual story she creates. Ciara lives in Edinburgh and usually has a camera in one hand and a cup of tea in the other. If you see her without these things, then she's likely on her way to get them. You can find her at @Ciara_Menzies and www.ciaramenzies.com